THE EYE OF THE PAINTER

AND THE ELEMENTS OF BEAUTY

ALSO BY ANDREW LOOMIS

THE EYE
OF THE PAINTER

AND THE ELEMENTS OF BEAUTY

Andrew Loomis

THE VIKING PRESS · NEW YORK

Acknowledgment is made to Time, Inc., for the color plates in this book.

Library of Congress catalog card number: 61-7388

LITHOGRAPHED IN THE U.S.A. BY POLYGRAPHIC COMPANY OF AMERICA

CONTENTS

ILLUSTRATIONS

THE EYE OF THE PAINTER

AND THE ELEMENTS OF BEAUTY

PROLOGUE

There can be little doubt that the chaotic condition of art today has caused confusion in the minds of artists, young and old. We are all asking: By what qualities, according to present standards, can a painting be judged? Is there still a solid foundation on which to base the teaching of art? Is art deteriorating, or is it being revitalized by new concepts?

It would seem that the most important problems now facing the artist are to achieve a clear personal understanding of what art is, to hew a pathway for his own creativeness, and to concentrate his efforts toward individual goals. He must realize that art can no longer be bound by theories other than individual theories; that is, it cannot be pigeonholed into prescribed method and practice. Art is having its growing pains. At long last, art has flung open its doors to individual creativeness in a way it has never done before. It has become a broader means of individual expression.

If we choose to become practicing artists today, we must widen the scope of art itself to take in all forms of creative expression. Art is no longer limited to traditional forms of painting and sculpture; it must be made an integral part of life as it is lived in the present and will be in the future. Art is also architecture, ceramics, industrial design, weaving, and textiles. It is a means of expression closely related to a new way of life.

Let us at once clear our minds of the concept that art is an "ism" or a cult. Such things exist within the complete concept but are only facets of a whole movement. When we can grasp the idea that art is an integral part of mankind itself, we need only to look back to see that it has existed since the dawn of intelligence. We find it in all peoples. Art is an expression of mankind's effort to make a better world, and to bring beauty into life in one form or another. It is a creative force, and as such will naturally align itself with the conditions and circumstances of the world in which man finds himself at any time. The present revolution in art is a logical result of a period of general revolt against traditions of all kinds.

At the bottom of the national and political crises today is the struggle for individual liberty and freedom of expression. It is therefore no coincidence that art has moved with the times and given the artist more freedom of expression than was ever known in the history of art.

There is always the danger that freedom can be abused. In art this means that the man without knowledge or ability is granted the same freedom as the skilled technician. Freedom is based on the assumption that the individual is morally and socially responsible, and to grant it to irresponsibility is like opening the doors to everyone who ever perpetrated a crime against society. The new-found freedom in art has set the pendulum of creativity swinging widely. There are painters wielding the brush who do not possess one iota of the fundamentals of art. We have "art" that would make the old masters jump back into their graves, were they to see it.

13

The good seems almost hopelessly mixed with the bad. Yet in spite of all that, art is now in a healthier state than it would have been if nothing had changed. Art cannot and should not stand still. That is stagnation. There is little danger that art will perish; only forms of art die. Confusion will eventually give way to order, and here and there new concepts of unquestionable value will develop. Meanwhile, instead of throwing out all the concepts and procedures of the past, let us search them for values that can be put to use today. Let us assemble a whole stock of knowledge gleaned from the past and add newer concepts, and in turn join these to the concepts that will come out of the future. Let us give art the benefit of the techniques of scientific exploration. The scientist does not throw away a theory until it has been proved false or valueless. To condemn the past because it is not part of the present would be as short-sighted as to stick only to the past for the sake of tradition. It would be short-sighted not to be alert to any new truth to add to our stock. Because certain forms of art can become passé, there is no reason to believe that basic knowledge is passé also.

Why not look at art as a stream, flowing by us like a river? Some has passed by, some is passing now, and there is still plenty that has not reached us. We might think of a single picture as one cup of water from this stream, reflecting in its surface some beautiful image, or representation of truth.

There are two satisfying and basic concepts by which artists have always worked and probably always will. Two-dimensional art—art rendered on a flat plane—will survive as ornamentation of one kind or another. Three-dimensional art will seek beauty of form. If we concede that ornamentation is the process of beautifying, then we find that beauty is the basis of both concepts. Mankind has from the beginning sought beauty, and by degrees added it to his environment. One man has the urge to create beauty, another the desire to seek it or own it, a desire which evidences itself every day in the selection of our possessions, in self-ornamentation, and in the beautifying of our surroundings. Whether it is creative or possessive, there is an innate desire for perfection, which broadly speaking is the basis for all progress. We seek to improve upon the efforts, accomplishments, and worldly goods of our neighbors. For the creative man there is instinctive pride in doing something better than others have done. On the possessive side, man wants the better product, the best craftsmanship, the better home, the beautiful wife. His desires in this direction seem to be limited only by the power to acquire, or the wherewithal to purchase. This drive toward creating beauty or possessing it is as basic to our lives as the air we breathe.

I cannot believe that the artist who establishes beauty as his fundamental approach to art can go very far wrong. No one denies that beauty is broad in scope, so broad that no single lifetime could encompass more than a small part of it. The great danger lies in allowing beauty to get bogged down in personal opinions, trends, and isms, in narrowing our individual understanding to the dogmas prated by the few. Beauty must be free, belonging individually to you and me, as far as we are capable of grasping it. Beauty is all around us, waiting to be discovered, and every artist interprets it on paper or canvas in his own particular way.

It is often asked how you can tell a good painting from a bad one. Vincent Price, the actor and art collector, answered this question well when he said, "A good painting is one that pleases you." If that is true, then the next question might be, "How do you paint a good picture?" I believe that there is a parallel answer here—paint in a manner that pleases you. Forget the other fellow and how he does it, unless you find his work particularly inspiring. Don't paint his way because of his arguments, his ambiguous explaining, and his salesmanship. The pleasure you feel in "doing" is the very basis of any individual technique that you may develop.

PROLOGUE

It is to your especial advantage that you may see beauty differently from the way others see it. This difference will help you select subjects that are attuned to your tastes. It will lead you on to new and exciting fields. The source of beauty is endless, but the true capturing of it is rare; it is a constant challenge.

In our search for subjects to paint we may go beyond nature and concentrate our attention merely on beauty of form, texture, or color. There is beauty to be found in pure geometrical forms, in spacing, in creating surfaces, planes, and abstract forms. We must therefore broaden our scope, and should we choose to work in the abstract, we will still find that beauty is our ultimate goal. Rather than condemning what we cannot agree with, we should take our full measure of the freedom allowed to all creative effort; we should do things as we believe they should be done, and give others the same freedom of ex-

pression. All art, to be worth its salt, must be individual. It must be creative. Realism can be creative, in the selection of the subject, and in rendering that subject as it is seen and felt by you as an individual. Whether your material exists in reality or not is not significant. You may paint an impression in broad terms or you may paint with great fidelity to detail, and either way achieve a fine creative work of art. The subject is not the picture; it is the way in which it is rendered that makes or breaks a work of art. Abstract art and realistic art are simply two different forms of approach, and there is no one who can say that one approach is any better than the other.

Art will always have its trends, derived from those who happen to be the greatest artisans of the moment. But the pendulum of creativeness is never still, since no two people can see with the same eyes or reason with the same brain. No two brains have identical receptivity or are motivated

The Gulf Stream by Winslow Homer, METROPOLITAN MUSEUM OF ART, NEW YORK CITY. Realism can be creative, in the selection of the subject, and in rendering that subject

15

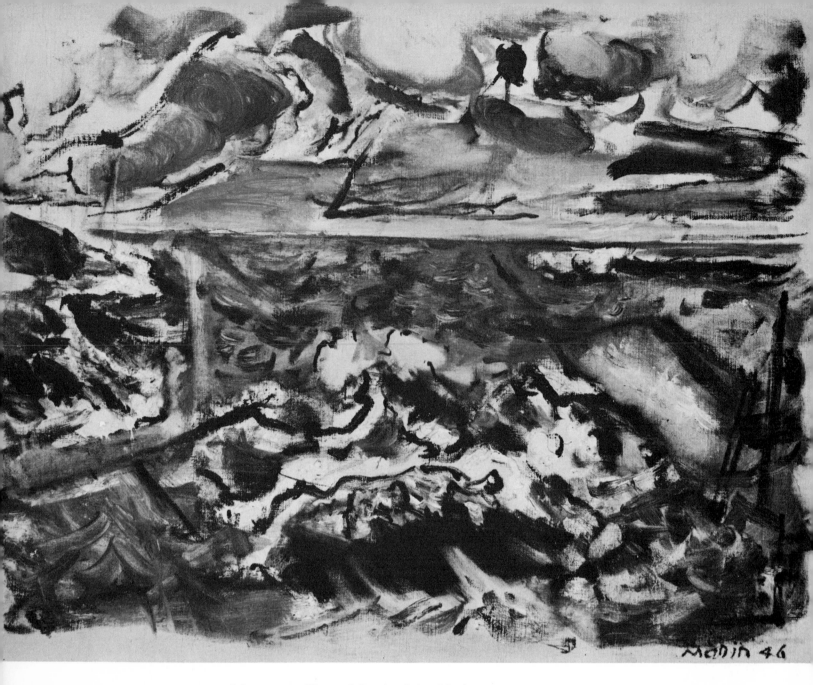

Movement, Sky and Sea by John Marin, THE DOWNTOWN GALLERY, NEW YORK CITY

You may paint an impression in broad terms or you may paint with great fidelity to detail, and either way achieve a fine creative work of art

16

Thinking Ahead by Yasuo Kuniyoshi, PHILLIPS MEMORIAL GALLERY, WASHINGTON, D. C.

and influenced by environment in exactly the same way. In fact, no two people could possibly start from scratch and paint identical pictures.

Today there seems to be a strong trend toward spontaneous, creative expression, without much regard for classical training. The creative urge is stronger than the will to study and acquire knowledge as the masters did in the past. Therefore we see paintings by men who have little or no academic knowledge, by men who are endeavoring to paint what they feel rather than what they see. We cannot deny them their right to express themselves in this manner, for it is entirely possible that a thing of beauty may be achieved by working from an emotional standpoint. In fact, the lack of one element may be more than compensated for by another, for, as everyone knows, there are many academic and expertly painted pictures that express so little emotion that they fail altogether as creative works of art. They can be trite and stiff and lacking altogether in both spirit and originality.

It is true, however, that the abstractionist without a classical training works against greater odds than the experienced realist does. He is like a man building a house without any knowledge of the carpenter's trade. All knowledge must come by way of experiment and innate craftsmanship, and he faces the extra hazard of being completely misunderstood. His creativeness must overshadow his technical faults, and lack of technical knowledge is extremely difficult to conceal for long.

So far as I know, there is no basic training by which a painter can learn to be an abstractionist —no fundamentals of drawing, values, color, or the rendering of form. I suggest that a young artist wishing to paint abstractions should be as well grounded in the fundamentals of technique as an objective painter must be. This has been true in the case of Picasso and many other modern artists. The student may then turn to the abstract if he chooses, with some hope of capturing the unity and organization, and finally the

beauty, that should be a part of any true work of art.

It is hardly possible—or wise—for an artist to decide at the outset of his career which type of painting he wants to do. The decision should be made later on when he is qualified by knowledge and training to go either way he chooses. One style is usually the outcome or, one might say, the refinement of another as the artist gains in experience and dexterity. Therefore he should not be impatient, but let his work evolve naturally, according to his ability and tastes.

In viewing gallery exhibitions today, we must understand that many canvases are hung without the remotest expectation of ever being sold. Many are exhibited for the sole purpose of educating the public to new concepts in art. We cannot tell at this point how successful this program of education will be, or even whether it is justified. But if the viewer bears in mind that many such works by modern artists are more in the nature of experiments than they are representations of an ideal, his attitude toward modern art is likely to be more lenient. My own opinion is that the canvases that will stand the test of time will be only those with inherent beauty, those which stand on their own merits and can be appreciated without high-sounding literary explanations by the avant-garde reviewer. Certainly people can and should be taught to accept new concepts, but in the final analysis beauty is judged by the eye and not the mind.

The soundest advice that can be given to any young painter is first and foremost to learn his craft well, to search constantly for beauty and new ways of expressing it, and, relating effort to inner convictions, to let his individual style evolve unhampered by any preconceived notions about how he should paint or what the critics are likely to say about it.

If I have, as I hope, convinced you that beauty still is and always will be the source of art, we can now turn our attention to the "whys" of beauty. Though perhaps no one can give a complete definition of what beauty is, we do come to understand that there are certain elements which combine to make beauty, whenever or wherever we find it. To recognize these elements and learn how they can serve us will greatly increase our prospects of achieving success as painters.

The elements of beauty are so well integrated that it is often very difficult to separate them for purposes of analysis. In discussing one principle or element it may be necessary to embrace another or even several others at the same time. Nevertheless, the attempt should be made to bring each one, separately, under our scrutiny. These are the basic twelve:

1. *Unity*. The "oneness" which brings all the pictorial qualities together into a single or whole expression; the organization of design, color, line, values, textures, and subject into a combined and total expression.

2. *Simplicity, or Clarity*. The subordination of all material and detail that is irrelevant to the main thought; the reduction of the subject into the fundamentals of design, form, and pattern.

3. *Design*. The over-all relationship of areas, form, and color. Design makes the picture.

4. *Proportion*. Harmonious relation of each subject and each part of the picture. Distortion is the opposite of proportion, though some distortion may be legitimate, where an idea or an emotion might need greater emphasis.

5. *Color*. This is one of the strongest elements of beauty, and in using it the artist cannot simply be guided by tastes, likes or dislikes. The relationship of color to values must be understood, as well as the basic principles of mixing and producing colors for realistic and harmonious effects.

6. *Rhythm*. Though this is often underestimated or misunderstood, it is a quality that contributes greatly to the beauty of a painting. There is rhythm in all animate and inanimate life, from the smallest forms to the cycles of the universe. Without it, form is static and lifeless. The repetition of similar colors or of lines or shapes of increasing or diminishing size will create rhythm in a painting just as it does in nature. For instance there is rhythm in the repeating lines of trees with their branches and leaves, or in the lines of a zebra's back, or in the petals or markings of a flower.

7. *Form*. The structure of form in relation to the whole is a fundamental art principle. Everything is either form or space (solid or void) and neither can exist without the other. A painting is said to have "form" when the shapes of the objects contained in it are well outlined, well composed, and properly contrasted with the open areas—such as a tree against the sky.

8. *Texture*. The rendering of surface. There is characteristic surface to all form, and this is as important as its structure. We cannot achieve true beauty by painting all form with the same type of surface, as if all things were made of the same material, which is precisely what happens too often in otherwise good painting.

9. *Values*. Values and color are inseparably dependent upon each other. Neither can be true or beautiful alone. The proper relationship of values creates the effects of light and contributes to the unity of the picture. Incorrect relationships can do more than anything else to destroy beauty.

10. *Quality of Light*. An element of prime importance. The quality of the light in a painting blends with the actual light fall-

ing upon the picture and becomes part of it. There are many kinds of light—indoor, outdoor sunlight, diffused light, reflected light. The source of light must be related to the modeling of form, to the kind and brilliancy of color, and to texture. Without a true understanding of light a picture can become mere planes of paint and canvas.

11. *Choice of Subject*. This offers the artist his greatest chance to exercise individual taste. The limitless sources of life and nature are his to tap and from them he can select, design, and produce a concentrated example of his own appreciation of beauty.

12. *Technique*. The means of expression rather than the expression itself. Technique includes understanding of surface and texture, knowledge of medium and its many methods of application. It is the personal rendering by which all the other elements are brought together.

This preview of the contents of the book should help to put us on common ground. It is certainly not my intention here to try to set myself or my work up as a shining example of the solution to the problems of the artist. But I do want to stress how important it is that every artist, be he professional or amateur, should recognize what his job is all about. I say again that there is no single form of art, or single formula for producing it. But when we find the elements that combine to create beauty in life, we can try to analyze and apply them to create beauty in our paintings. Beauty is not the special property of the artist. Beauty is perhaps just as evident to others, who may lack the knowledge and ability to re-create it. The rhythm and grace of an animal must be just as apparent to the lover of animals as to the artist. The difference is that we try to find out what makes the rhythm and grace in terms of line and proportion, so that our renderings are true and convincing.

The artist will do well to direct his efforts toward pleasing the viewer rather than the critics, for the viewer is the ultimate purchaser, and I assume that most artists are interested in selling their work. While art dealers have done a great deal of exploitation, and monetary values of paintings have often been pushed to astronomical figures, in most cases the artists themselves have never lived to receive these benefits. Today good art can find a good market, in commercial fields as well as in the field of "fine art." Paintings of the easel type, for hanging on the wall, will seldom bring the financial rewards that come from illustration, advertising, and other commercial work. But we have, fortunately, reached a stage where the finest art is often used for commercial purposes. Industry is now providing a new outlet for fine art, and the artist bend upon perfecting his craft to the utmost is no longer considered too good for such a market, as was once believed.

While the strictly commercial artist may still have to work within limitations set by the purchasing agency or the ultimate user, such limits are being greatly broadened, and the work of easel painters has been used in many advertising campaigns.

This development has come about gradually, aided by the introduction of color photography into commercial fields. When exact detail is important to the sale of the advertised product, the advertiser naturally turns to photography and is likely to do so for some time. Where no tangible product can be pictured, as in advertising insurance, services, industrial prestige, and in institutional advertising in general, a market for fine art has developed. Magazine illustration continues to provide a market for the artist, partly because the use of paintings helps differentiate fiction from factual articles. For the latter, photographs are ordinarily used to substantiate the text.

It is foolish for the artist to try to compete with

the camera in achieving fidelity of detail. Better that he use his creative and imaginative powers and direct his efforts toward design. Even if he uses a camera for working material, the artist can still concentrate upon the things that a camera cannot do; he can subordinate and eliminate, design and rearrange, simplify and take other liberties to project his idea more forcefully.

The professional artist should prepare for his profession by as thorough training as possible, in art schools and classes, or from any sources he can find available. It is a fallacy that no training is necessary in order to make a living at drawing or painting. The fact that we may often see pictures in exhibitions that show no apparent talent, knowledge, or ability, and which we feel certain that we could equal or better, has nothing to do with the case. Much of the art exhibited today would not buy a sack of potatoes.

Progress and development in art must always be the progress and development of the individual. One artist can help others to a degree only. He can call attention to facts that, over a period of effort, he has found to be true. He can point out relationships that he has found to exist. He can show that colors will mix with definite result, that values will unify and organize a subject. This is what I hope to do in this book. If I can show the beginner a few "hows" and "whys," I will have accomplished my purpose.

The Bull Fight by Francisco Goya, METROPOLITAN MUSEUM OF ART, NEW YORK CITY. A lightly sketched-in figure can often look more alive and real than one that has been painted in great detail

I. SEEING WITH THE PAINTER'S EYE

The artist's first step toward the ultimate beauty, unity, and organization of painting is learning to see everything in pictorial terms. This will mean the closest possible unification between the eye, the hand, and the medium with which we have chosen to work. In time most artists find that the hand automatically works with the eye even to the mixing and application of medium. In fact, artists often are surprised—and delighted—to discover that they have unconsciously used a certain technique to express exactly the impression they had intended. The artist either puts down a suggestion of what he sees, or the object as he sees it, being at the moment unconcerned with technique. Technique is thus a result rather than a conscious manner of stroke. Yet every artist in time develops a technical approach, if he is patient and has faith in his vision and emotional reaction.

Of course, we all see shining examples of technique, some of which we admire very much, and which the young especially—and sometimes the old—are tempted to copy for technique's sake alone. As a result technique actually gets in our way and we end up by not seeing the subject we are painting truly and often overlook many of the other essential elements of painting as well.

When a man is thinking in terms of technique he probably is not giving his best attention to values, relationships, or even color. He is thinking about the strokes he is making and not very much else. Technique is a strong indication of individuality, and, if you allow it to do so, it will get into your work subconsciously. It is much like handwriting, of which no two specimens are exactly alike.

The best advice I can offer is to paint what you see as you see it. And if you can suggest an object or a scene so that it is convincing, that may even be better than completely boning it out. In a landscape, for instance, a lightly sketched-in figure can often look more alive and real than one that has been painted in great detail. The truth is that we can quite easily train the eye to see as we want it to see; in fact it has already been trained to do this. We can skim through a crowd and spot the face we are looking for, and hardly be conscious of any of the other faces there. If we are painting warm sunlight, we may see it warm, possibly warmer than it actually is. If we are drawing in outline we see in outline, and are only faintly aware of anything else. If we are rendering a subject in tone, we begin to see values and relationships that we had not noticed before. In the first case we are really looking primarily at outline and see everything else as secondary; in the second case, mass and tone become of primary importance to us and edges and outlines more incidental. When we look for color, we must somehow also keep values or tone very closely associated with it, and here is where the training of the eye begins.

The tendency to see only one thing or aspect of a scene at a time is something we must educate

23

our eyes not to do. Too many pictures are started with line only, then the outlines are filled in with tone, without regard to the real edge, or what the tone is doing, or what its relationship is to other tones. Tone and color are applied in a more or less schoolbook manner, simply by filling areas between outlined limits. This is not painting in the true sense.

The experienced painter studies his subject in all its aspects. The more he can see the total effect before he starts, the better the painting will be. He will look at mass with its edges or outlines, seeing the mass in its value and color, and according to its relationship to other masses and colors. He does not single out one thing at a time, for all these things are closely connected and belong to or affect one another.

We may start a picture in outline, but only after we have carefully noted where that outline is going to merge and lose itself in other tone. We may even indicate this on our drawing with short lines across the edge, which means that this edge is to be soft or lost. If we draw a hard outline around everything, the chances are that we will forget all about the true edges and accept the hard edges we have set down. Then we end with a tight, hard picture with no freedom of approach, one that is unimaginative and not particularly creative. Such a picture is really a colored drawing. Working from photographs has a tendency to increase this tightness and hardness. We cannot see the life image; we simply copy what a sharp lens has recorded, putting in every detail.

Before you look at your subject, before you lay a hand on the canvas, stop and realize that any picture starts as a flat tone (the canvas) which is eventually broken up into more tones. Thus a pattern of arrangement of masses and spots is created. This is actually the first thing you should train your eyes to see—the picture as a whole with as much identification as possible of the pattern or design. You should decide where the borders of the picture will be, and its shape and dimensions. The habit of roughing out patterns or composition in miniature is a good one.

Learning to see your subject in terms of simple masses with a general relationship to one another in color and value is the first law of good painting. We can train our eyes to see mass without detail by deciding what the general value and colors are to be. Then, later on, we can raise the value for the highlights and lower it for the shadows. What we are really seeking in this manner is the approximate middle tone of the area or mass, and this we set down quite flatly in simple poster terms. In cases where you want to maintain the underdrawing, which is usually done with charcoal and fixed, or is a light drawing gone over with waterproof India ink, you can use thin turpentine washes over the drawing so that it shows through. It is even better to learn to draw within the mass, establishing planes, halftones, accents, highlights, or texture as you develop the picture.

To see the general tone of the mass with less detail, try squinting the eyes and looking through the lashes.

From the very beginning, line up the values in the order in which they appear. Look for the lightest value and label it number one; the next value will be number two, and so on until you establish about eight gradations. Here we are training the eye to see values in relationship to one another in the black and white scale. Areas of the same value may appear lighter or darker than they actually are because of a neighboring color. A light yellow may seem much lighter and brighter than a light blue, although they have the same black and white ratio in the value scale. To recognize this takes a certain amount of training.

Though we do and must draw as we paint, let us think of drawing as associated with outline, and painting as associated with mass values and color. We do not want a painting to turn out to be a drawing, nor do we want a drawing to become a colored-over excuse for a painting. Much poor art is neither true drawing nor true painting, but an unhappy confusion of both. A good draw-

1. If we copy nature as we find her, our drawing will be something like Number 1. Tracing an actual photo would be much the same.

2. Block in the forms in simple terms like this, eliminating detail.

3. This shows what the masses would look like if Number 1 were to be accepted with every form "as is."

4. In finishing Number 2 more thought is given to pattern and design, less to edges and outlines.

5. Further simplification of Number 4.

6. Here realism is abandoned for the sake of pure design. Only a slight identification of subject remains. We may call this an abstract interpretation.

7. In this rendering, edges are more clearly defined.

8. With vertical and horizontal lines the design becomes even more abstract and in some respects even more effective.

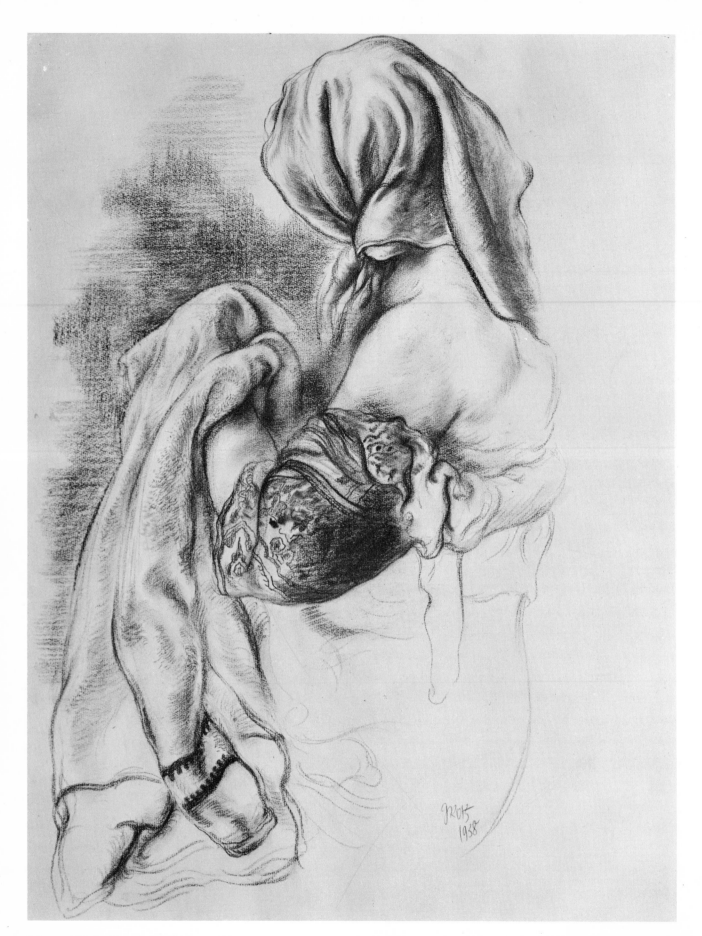

Figure With Shawl by George Grosz, WALKER GALLERIES, NEW YORK CITY. Art training usually starts with drawing, for the student must first train his eyes to proportion, and go as far as he can with form in a simple black and white medium

ing should remain drawing by having the structure and outline very much in evidence, and leaving it at that. A good painting should stress tone and pattern with an intermingling of forms and edges, with some edges stressed and others subordinated. Line as line does not belong in painting, for outlines do not actually exist in nature, which is what a painting, or a classical painting, at any rate, attempts to represent as closely as possible. In nature we see only contours and edges. Forms are defined by values appearing one against another, and there is no need to represent these divisions in any other way. However, in drawing we have no other way to define an edge or the limits of the forms before us, except in line.

This difference between drawing and painting should be firmly understood. Good drawing, of course, underlies good painting, but the essence of good painting goes beyond edges and contours into the rendering of the solid form as it appears in a given light, in its color and texture, surrounded by space and atmosphere. Such qualities cannot be reached in a subject where all units and parts are separated by hard outline, or completely identified edges around everything.

Art training usually starts with drawing, for the student must first train his eyes to proportion, and go as far as he can with form in a simple black and white medium. But he will not see true values until he starts to paint.

We train our eyes to perspective largely by learning the rudiments of it, and recognizing the perspective before us as belonging to the law of optics. Perspective is actually the science of drawing form and space as it appears to the eye, as opposed to mechanical projection drawing which renders form on a flat plane or planes in actual dimension. In order to paint we must know how to scale form and proportion in space; we must understand the complete principle of the eye-level or horizon which is the cornerstone of all accurate representations involving perspective.

In order to differentiate painting and drawing

to his students, the late Charles Hawthorne, one of the great American painters and instructors, made his students start their canvases in reverse order. Instead of drawing the usual outline, they started with patches of tone and color and fitted them together in the best proportion they could. His idea was that they could eventually learn to draw and get subjects designed within the canvas shape, but that the ability to see things together, in relationship of tone and color, was far more important. It really did not matter too much to him if the subject got onto the canvas minus hands or feet; the main thing was to learn to paint by educating the eye.

It is not a bad idea for the artist to make this kind of experiment. Set up a still life, and without any preliminary drawing, start painting in areas and masses of tone and color; then in these masses develop the form. Drawing can be easily corrected in oil when it is dry. Where edges merge or are very close in value, keep them lost or soft. Where they stand out in contrast, make them so. If you have never worked this way it may seem difficult, for there are no lines to work up to; they will have to be established later as edges, or lack of edge. This is one of the best ways of training the eye.

There is an in-between approach to drawing, which can be beautiful and which still qualifies as drawing. That is combining massed shadow with outline. While we do not attempt all the subtleties of modeling and light and shadow, we do delineate a strong effect of light and shadow, more as it would be seen in very strong light, the lights being white or the tone of the paper, and the darks or shadows in simple areas being very dark or black. If the drawing is made on tone paper, white may be added with startling effects. Actually this means drawing in about three or four tones.

There have been illustrators and commercial artists whose work was basically drawing in paint, and definitely on the side of drawing. Outstanding among these was J. C. Leyendecker. How-

TAKING YOUR CANVAS OUTDOORS
FOR DIRECT PAINTING OF THE LANDSCAPE

AREA BEYOND PAINTING

LEFT EDGE OF PICTURE

HORIZON

EYE
A

PICTURE BASELINE

6 FT.

B

PICTURE BASELINE ON THE GROUND

GROUNDLINE BELOW PICTURE

MIDDLE LINE

C

RIGHT EDGE OF PICTURE

AREA BEYOND PAINTING

STATION POINT

About 10 ft. of actual width at baseline of picture.

Few artists ever stop to realize that in outdoor painting they are really painting a huge pie-shaped slice of the stretch of landscape before them. The importance of realizing this is manifold.

First, the baseline of the painting represents comparatively few feet, while the distance may represent miles across the picture. In the diagram above, note that the baseline of the picture represents only about ten feet. Approximate this line in front of you by sighting beyond the bottom corners of your canvas to the ground with your eye opposite the middle line of your canvas. (AB and AC). Draw foreground material between B and C. You can lay stones at the points B and C and sight in vertical lines above them to find how much distance you should include. The vertical lines are the right and left edges of your painting. These lines actually fan out to the horizon and distance. This keeps the foreground in correct relation to the distance. The horizon of the picture should be at the eye-level of the painter, and you will find it easiest to paint if you set your canvas so the two coincide.

Thus, by first establishing the actual area of landscape to be incorporated into your canvas you can paint all material the same size as you see it.

THREE-DIMENSIONAL EYE TRAINING

The contours of any object will fit within a rectangle or box. By studying the shape of the object, we can visualize a box around it of appropriate proportions. First sketch the box, then draw the object to fit within the box, in similar perspective. You thus train your eye to see the solidity of the form, rather than just its contours. The child usually draws contours without perspective.

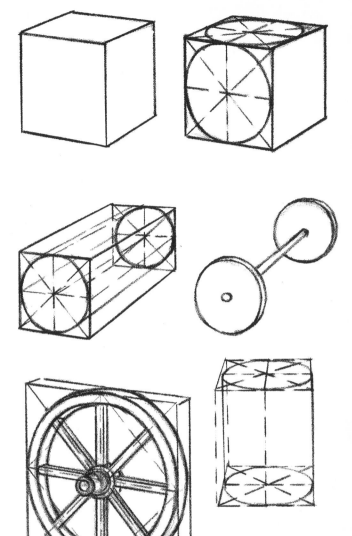

This is particularly helpful when we are drawing round objects. It also aids us in drawing correct and true ellipses in good perspective as related to the eye-level at which we are viewing the object. Everything in a picture should be drawn from a single viewpoint or eye-level.

If you learn to visualize the box, you won't have much difficulty in rendering the object in correct proportion. Try to locate the corners of the box, just where they would appear around the object. This is not always as simple as it may seem.

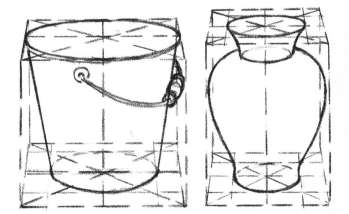

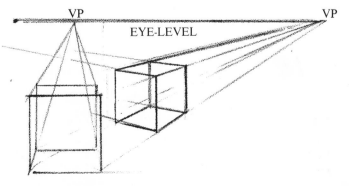

SEE AND MENTALLY DRAW THE IMAGE OF A CLOSE-FITTING BOX AS YOU STUDY THE FORM BEFORE YOU. IT WILL HELP TO ESTABLISH TRUE PERSPECTIVE.

29

ever, I doubt if a close imitation of his style would sell today. McClelland Barclay used strong outline in his later work to good effect, as did Herbert Paus, but the appeal in the work of these men really came from design, pattern, and color. There are many styles between true painting and good drawing which are used by commercial artists. The danger lies in being tricky, rather than doing work of basic excellence. Tricky approaches can be easily copied or plagiarized, whereas pictures based on sound knowledge and the individuality of the artist are hard to imitate.

In order to train the eye toward arrangement, pattern, and good composition the artist can begin in a more or less abstract way to play with patterns in miniature. Without worrying about subjects, he may simply try to spot masses and shapes of three or four different values within a squared-off rectangle. Everyone has an inherent sense of balance and order which varies immensely with the individual. But this sense must be developed by experiment, just as vision is by practice. You are the only one who can do it. Reading books on composition can be helpful, but in the end your own taste and selectiveness will plan your pictures.

The eye must also be trained to organize what it sees in terms of a composition. Nature has a way of strewing her material in a haphazard fashion around the surface of the earth. With wind and water, frost, and all the other elements working over the surface it gets to be a rather mixed-up affair. But an intelligent approach can be developed as we come to understand nature. What we see are effects due for the most part to causes that are often less evident. If we can grasp the cause, it helps us greatly in understanding the effect. Pictures are really effects.

Suppose we are looking at a landscape. Assume for the moment that it is a desert scene. Before us is a profusion of forms, surfaces, and shapes of light and shadow. We can analyze the scene in a way that greatly helps us to paint it. First let us try to determine the causes that pro-

duced the effects we see. Understanding them will give character and a convincing quality to our picture. As we look at the ground we can trace what water courses and floods have done to the surface. Here they have made grooves and channels in the surface. There sediment has been deposited in shapes that still define the flow. Rocks have been scraped and torn away, others show grinding by water, wind, and sand. We follow the slope by which the water came, back perhaps to the distant mountains where melting snow even more than rain must have carved the effects we see. We look for desert growth: is there still some green, some vitality in it that through ages has learned to survive drought. What color is it? Are there lesser plants that are parched? What is the nature of the soil and its general color? How does it differ from the buttes and terraces which rise above it? Does the whole scene seem lighter or darker than the sky?

Now we begin to look for arrangements. How can we utilize that sweep of the dry wash? Would it be better if we were to move those bushes and trees a little to the left or right? Have we nice patterns of light and shadows? We note the direction of the sun, and the brightest planes which must stay at right angles to the source of light. We list our values from the lightest to darkest by comparing them and realize that we must stick to this sequence. If we are looking into the light, the sky will probably be brighter than we can paint it. So we must make all the values a tone or two darker than we see them, to establish the same scale but in a lower key.

We know the distant mountain is cool in color because the same atmosphere which appears blue in the sky is between us and that mountain, dropping a veil of blue over the actual or local color.

Now if the scene is crowded and "busy," with rocks, forms, lights and shadows, we seek to simplify the profusion by actually eliminating some material, and grouping the rest of it into patterns. It takes very little to make an effective picture—nature usually provides too much. We get out a pencil and pad and rough out several small compositions. If one of them pleases us, we are ready to make a sketch.

This is educating the eye by means of the material before it and the brain behind it. We have thought about something more than outlined shapes and paint strokes. Each time you study nature you will gain additional working knowledge if you insist upon sizing up causes and effects, and then set them down, instead of slavishly copying what you see as you might copy a photograph. You cannot put into the picture everything that is there before you, in all its overabundance of irrelevant detail and literal fact, and still paint a good picture. You might better use your camera. You are making a lens of your eye and an empty box of your head, doing the same thing the camera does.

To help in the process of elimination, first paint a very small color sketch. This should be so small that you cannot possibly include all the intricate detail, but must settle for mass and general planes. Then make a larger sketch, checking with the small one and leaving out much of the material you were forced to omit from it. Start with the masses. When the mass becomes identified enough to be convincing as ground, foliage, rock, or cloud, try to leave it. You can always see more detail than you can paint, and you can watch a picture that started out as a striking and positive approach deteriorate into a commonplace, over-worked nothing! How many times have we all done it? And we will keep on doing it until we learn the hard way that nature should be used as a source only, and that enough detail is enough.

There are a few tried and true and generally accepted facts about outdoor painting, and to look for them helps train the eye. The sky is ordinarily the lightest pattern or mass, unless there is a very bright pattern of buildings or other material that is white or nearly so.

The next lightest mass is usually the ground. This gets the direct light of the sun, on a more or less flat plane. The third value will be found in sloping planes, slanting away from the light source, such as mountains, roofs, banks, and so forth. The darkest patterns for the most part are found in the uprights, such as trees, cliffs, or anything that casts a shadow toward the ground.

You will usually find that all shadows go down in scale relative to the lights. This means that the lightest tone in the shadow will be found next to the lightest tone in the light, the next darker tone in the shadow will be on the next lower tone in the light, and so on down to the darkest object in the light, which naturally has the darkest shadow. The lightest shadow ordinarily starts about the middle of the scale or very little above it. This means that white normally has a shadow about middle tone, or only slightly above, and that all the lights and shadows scale down from there in proper sequence. We must not forget, however, that some shadows may be lightened from their natural sequence, because of light reflected from the ground or cast from some light surface nearby.

Setting up a scale of values for your picture helps you to train your eye to see color in a pictorial sense. We all can see colors and their tints; we all can name them fairly accurately as long as they are more or less pure color. But pictorially we get into many nameless colors which are muted and softened as a result of the kind of light or atmosphere in which they appear. Pictorially color is true only when its value is right, when its warmness or coolness is right in relation to the neighboring color. We cannot mix sky color or ground color, foliage color or even flesh color and put it into a tube. Flesh under a blue sky and within the shade appears totally different from the same flesh seen in warm sunlight. The reflected blue light of the sky, or the warm light of the sun, has altered the local or actual color of the flesh and made it relative to all its surroundings.

We look for cause and effect in color, as well as in form and other pictorial qualities. If there is

31

ORGANIZATION AND GROUPING

The complexity and overabundance of form, texture, and material in nature is frustrating and confusing unless some attempt is made to bring about order. This means simplification, elimination, and grouping into pattern. The two pictures at left show literal renderings of a landscape as they might appear in a photograph; the versions at right show how organization of the same forms results in a better picture.

Storm by Dean Fausett, KRAUSHAAR GALLERIES, NEW YORK CITY.   The sky is ordinarily the lightest pattern or mass . . . the next lightest mass is usually the ground . . . the third value will be found in sloping planes, slanting away from the light source

bright sunlight on green grass, the bright green is reflected upward to reach the underplane of any form above it. It may also reflect upward into a shadow area as, for example, the shadow side of a barn. At the same time the blue of the sky may be hitting the same plane. So the shadow will be warm at the bottom and cooler at the top, and it will also be affected by the local color of the barn itself.

Training the eye of the artist is to a large extent providing information as to what to look for. No one man can make as many observations and pictorial discoveries on his own as have been made by artists collectively. But each one will make for himself many discoveries that he will then be able to recognize in other men's work. These things are rarely learned by copying, but by direct contact with nature, which is the way artists of all time have learned them.

Beauty does not exist for us until we become conscious of it. To some people all things exist more or less as groups—trees, flowers, animals, automobiles—each group looks more or less alike until one gets particularly interested in a subject and makes a study of it. Should you become interested, in fine automobiles then you will see each car individually, as a unit and with a character of its own. This is the way the eye of the artist must work. He must see a tree as an individual tree, its growth, its particular formations and branches, the groups of leafy forms which make it that tree and no other. Nicholai Feschin told one of his students, "Paint the apple, not an apple." Frederic Remington painted many scenes involving Indians, but if he painted an Apache it was an Apache, not just an Indian. Such differences are important and lend authority to a painting.

II. "WHAT SHALL I PAINT?"

Superfluous as this question may sound, it poses the biggest problem an artist faces. One reason many artists prefer commercial work is that the subject is usually settled upon before the artist is called in. In most cases there is material to work from, at least in the form of layouts, sketches, and theme. If the artist is required to prepare his own working material, he has but to call in his model, get out his camera, go to his files for suggestions, and then proceed with the job. This practice relieves him of the need of finding subjects, but it also limits him. The chances are that he will build his picture according to the client's tastes and wishes rather than his own; he must deliberately subordinate himself and much of his own creativeness to someone else's demands.

That is why many commercial artists turn to fine art in their later years, after the financial pressures have lessened. But the step is actually a big one. The artist who has never exercised his creative ability beyond the demands of an assignment may find himself at a loss for ideas, for avenues of expression for that extra creativeness that is required to become wholly original. To search for subjects without regard for a preconditioned cash value is something new. Painting solely for the sake of beauty and craftsmanship and the "joy of doing" is unfamiliar. If, on the other hand, he has planned throughout his career for this well-earned day of freedom, he will be armed with new ambitions, relieved of pressures and tensions, with the door open to new experience and new goals to reach for.

This is not to suggest that commercial art cannot be beautiful, or even qualify as fine art. The point is, has the artist, during his career of painting for other people, done any painting for himself? Has he attempted to express himself alone, has he tried to achieve the finest craftsmanship of which he is capable, with no thought of money in the process? Has he tried to show his work in noncommercial exhibitions?

If he has, the step will not be so great. That is why, in my belief, every artist should keep reaching above himself. He should go out and acquaint himself with nature. He should sketch. He should do some of the things he wants to do, rather than do only those he is being paid to do. Every young artist should realize that his commercial career inevitably reaches a peak, from which it must go down, since style trends constantly change as advertisers and agencies search for something new and different. The higher a man goes, and the more of his work that appears, the more certain it is that his output will be replaced by another's to keep up with the desire for change. Some men are capable of changing with the times, prolonging their usefulness, but eventually all must bow to the young, the new, and the different. This is one of the motivating reasons for this book—to urge the artist, young or old, to think always in terms of beauty, of improvement, of the finest craftsmanship of which he is capable.

35

In the process of developing, one must cheerfully accept limitations, but by doing so one earns the right to the day of freedom. When that day comes, instead of feeling that you are through, how much more wonderful to feel that you are free! How a man plans for that day is his own business. But there are always new fields to conquer if he is prepared. I hope I can instill in the reader an awareness that his personal search for beauty is his best stock in trade. Not only does it improve his work, thus increasing his income and bringing interest and happiness in the doing, but it also builds up a reservoir of accomplishment and well-being for the whole of his life. There is no end to the search, no end to the source, no end to the accomplishment. There is no age limit to the start or finish other than the span of life itself.

There are many ways of finding or preparing material for painting. Let me mention some of them. One of the best ways is to build up a file of subjects that interest you. Even though these in a sense are "copy," the same kind that is used in commercial work, they do not need to be literally copied and they provide necessary information. This file may contain clippings, postcards showing interesting places, transparencies and photographs you have taken yourself, art reproductions that you can learn from, roughs and compositions you have made up in your spare time, or actual pencil sketches and notations you have made. When you get out in your car, or during vacations, always have your camera and sketchbook with you.

If you have the time and energy, try making direct color sketches outdoors. Because light and weather conditions change so fast, it is seldom practical to attempt large paintings in the open, unless the spot can be revisited under the same conditions. Then there is the hazard of wind or rain. If your easel blows over, it is usually—alas—with the canvas face down. But you *can* make sketches under almost any and all conditions.

Sometimes you see by chance a scene that strikes you as startling and effective. If you have time for nothing else, at least jot down a description of the general composition and color, and any other notes that will be helpful in re-creating the scene in your studio later on. Put these in your file of "Subjects to Paint."

You can make a simple "finder" by cutting a small opening in a black card, in about the proportions you prefer to paint. Carry it in your coat pocket. Looking through this finder as your eyes range over a particularly "paintable" view can help enormously in settling on the most suitable area to choose for a landscape composition.

Develop the habit of drawing abstract patterns and shapes within a small rectangle. Three or four values are enough. If these suggest a subject, rough one out, and save it.

Painting from life is always better than faking. If time is limited, you can set up a still life. The more unusual the setup, the more varied the material, the more interesting the picture. Portrait studies are always possible, interesting, and a means of increasing your skill.

You will be more interested in developing the material you have prepared yourself, or seen for yourself, than in using what you are given for a job. Besides training the eye to see the material before you, you can train yourself to be on the alert for material in any shape or form. If you have the desire to paint, now or later on, you will need material to work from. A file of material waiting to be used is the best "fresher-upper" an artist can have—especially if the last job did not go too well. A still life which contains no faking is a great restorer of confidence in your ability.

Go to art exhibitions; see what is being done. If you are interested in abstract art, here is a whole new field for experiment, in which you can play with design and color and create at will. If some abstract art appears ugly to you, see if you can do something more beautiful. You have the whole range of the spectrum. Your design may be geometrical or free-form. You can take concrete or identifiable form, and reduce it to the abstract.

Pears and Pewter by Luigi Lucioni, THE METROPOLITAN MUSEUM OF
ART, NEW YORK CITY.   Painting from life is always better than faking.
If time is limited, you can set up a still life

Egg Beater V by Stuart Davis, THE MUSEUM OF MODERN ART, NEW YORK CITY.   If you are interested in abstract art, here is a whole new field for experiment, in which you can play with design and color and create at will

"WHAT SHALL I PAINT?"

A man who employs such freedom in his spare-time experiments may easily find that he can apply some of his personal discoveries in his everyday work, and thus improve it.

There is one thing we must not do, and that is to let time go by without doing anything. Nothing can lead to such frustration and discouragement. One may be tempted to look forward to the day when one is rid of present responsibilities with nothing but idle freedom ahead, but idle freedom is its own worst enemy. Where there is no achievement there is little happiness.

In choosing a subject let us give great consideration to simplicity. Not only is a simple subject more within the scope of the average artist, but the result, even from the best of painters, will be more forceful and telling. We have learned from poster art that simplicity will make a design "carry" when viewed from a greater distance. It is safe to say that the smaller the picture, the simpler the design should be. A painting may be considered most effective if the viewer can stand at least ten feet away and get the full impact. If it is exhibited in a gallery, the effect should carry at least twenty to thirty feet.

It follows that subjects with intricate pattern and detail should be painted on a large canvas, but even in larger pictures simple patterns stand out most effectively. Therefore the artist should select his subject with this in mind. He has the choice either of simplifying the material he includes or of eliminating enough material to simplify the picture. Wide-vista subjects must usually be simplified much more than more intimate close-ups. In landscape, sometimes whole mountains may be eliminated, especially when they occur in series, for the sake of the larger, more dominant ones. In busy skies, about half the clouds may give place to fewer and larger ones. Sometimes as much as two-thirds of the scattered material may be eliminated without apparent loss. The aim of the artist is not to make a complete record of the place, but to create a beautiful canvas.

The student is urged to experiment with designing pure pattern without reference to actual material or subject. This can be done as well in black and white as in color, and is an excellent way of developing a "feel" for design.

With any of the black-and-white mediums use for a background a white, gray, or black paper. Chalk may be used on the darker papers. Now

White Canadian Barn, No. 2 by Georgia O'Keeffe, THE MUSEUM OF MODERN ART, NEW YORK CITY.   Not only is a simple subject more within the scope of the average artist, but the result, even from the best of painters, will be more forceful and telling

simply start to produce interlacing patterns of about four values. The paper background may be the dominant pattern. Try to balance one area with another. Try large, simple patterns at first, and then some that are a little more intricate. These pattern sketches need be no larger than three by four inches. Though you start these without any particular subject in mind, they will often suggest subjects. Try not to have any two areas of pattern the same size or shape.

When we speak of three or four values of pattern this does not mean distinct and separated *areas* of pattern. If we have four spotted or interlacing patterns, they may be cut up into as many separated areas as we wish, and still be considered a four-value pattern. One pattern may jump over another, be surrounded by or placed against another. One pattern may be quite simple, and another considerably broken up. You may do anything you like to create design, but keep it all in about four values.

Some of the best pictures start out this way. If your design suggests something, try working it out with further manipulation into the kind of subject it suggests. This is an abstract approach to which realism is added later. You might work out the design with colored pencils, crayons, or chalk. Once in a while you will come up with a little gem. Save these for your subject file; they can be life-savers.

Another trick which can be a help in finding subjects is to take your palette scrapings and dab them on a piece of paper, fairly close together. Fold the paper and step on it to squeeze and blend the palette scrapings together. They will penetrate the absorbent paper. Then with your palette knife, scrape off the surplus paint. The design will remain as it first penetrated the paper. Now take your little finder and move it over the colored areas. With a pencil, trace around the opening and mark off the little compositions that are interesting. Then cut these out and mount them on gray or black paper. You will find some accidental compositions that are unusual and beautiful and they can be developed into whatever subjects they suggest.

There are other ways of arriving at abstract designs which often lead to suggestions for compositions and subjects. Take two sheets of gray paper, one lighter than the other, a black sheet, and a white one. Tear these into different-sized pieces, shake them up in a box, then lay a finder over them as they happened to fall. If you get a good design, sketch in on a pad beside the box with a soft lead pencil. Or you can fill the bottom of a box with scraps of colored papers, shake them, and lay your finder over them. You may get some very interesting patterns of color.

Try moving a finder over a large photograph. You may either choose an actual bit of the subject for a composition—which may be much more interesting than the whole—or by turning the finder and moving it around, discover some fascinating abstract patterns.

You may come across a good color subject in a magazine, perhaps one with a fairly large and complete figure. Run the small finder over the head and shoulders and an idea for a portrait may be the result. These may also be interesting accessories in a large picture which, when cut down to a smaller surrounding area by the finder, suggest excellent still lifes.

I know one artist who carries a small black box around with him. It has a small round hole in the back, and a rectangular one, also quite small, in the front, so that he can look through the small aperture in the back and on through the front opening, which squares off the view. This is like a camera finder and is a tremendous aid in picking out nice arrangements. It also helps to line up the values of the subject, which are discussed later.

A most interesting way to create abstract pictures is to take a color print and try to create a design out of those colors only. Build your own shapes and patterns, or, if you wish, try to reduce

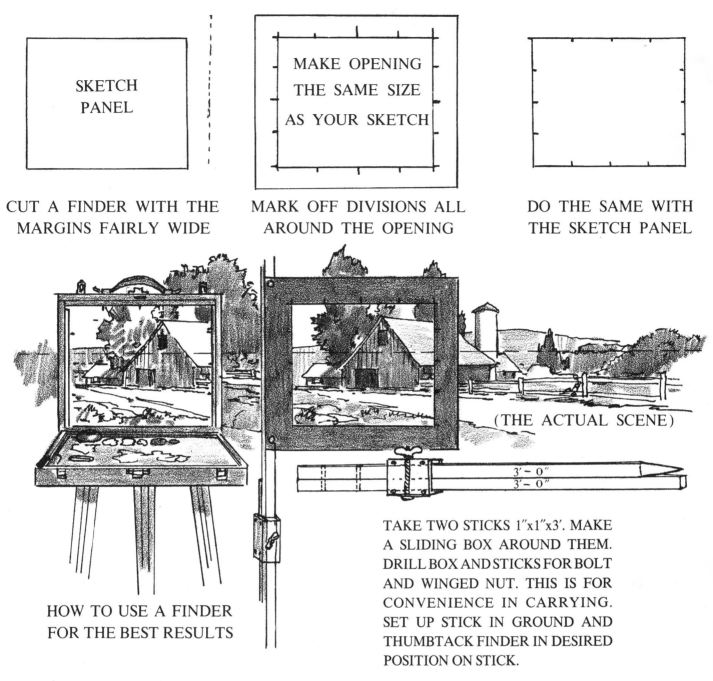

SKETCH
PANEL

CUT A FINDER WITH THE
MARGINS FAIRLY WIDE

MAKE OPENING
THE SAME SIZE
AS YOUR SKETCH

MARK OFF DIVISIONS ALL
AROUND THE OPENING

DO THE SAME WITH
THE SKETCH PANEL

(THE ACTUAL SCENE)

3'-0"
3'-0"

HOW TO USE A FINDER
FOR THE BEST RESULTS

TAKE TWO STICKS 1"x1"x3'. MAKE
A SLIDING BOX AROUND THEM.
DRILL BOX AND STICKS FOR BOLT
AND WINGED NUT. THIS IS FOR
CONVENIENCE IN CARRYING.
SET UP STICK IN GROUND AND
THUMBTACK FINDER IN DESIRED
POSITION ON STICK.

A small finder held fairly close to the eye is excellent for finding subjects. However, once a subject is decided upon, it is more helpful to have one with an opening exactly the same size as your sketch. This can be thumbtacked to a stick next to the sketchbox. Place this so the two are aligned, as shown above. In this manner you can keep viewing the real scene as you make your sketch, and you will find it easier to draw all the objects in correct scale and proportion. The image is fairly constant if you keep the head in the same position for both viewing and painting.

Pigeon by Zoltan Sepeshy, MIDTOWN GALLERIES, NEW YORK CITY.
Children at the seashore can be a most attractive subject

the existing shapes into geometrical forms and planes. Use no perspective, and little or no modeling of form. Work only for beautiful color arrangement and striking design. If there is harmony of color in the material, you can thus get it into your design. Let one color dominate, and the rest play against it.

Pictures that attempt to tell a story are a different form of art, which might better be called illustration, but there is no reason why they can-

not be beautiful. Children at the seashore can be a most attractive subject. Animals have their place in art. Motherhood has always been an important theme. Other themes can be taken from various human activities, such as sports, the circus, farm life, and city streets. Old barns, quaint houses, factories can all be worthy subjects.

We can run through the category of human emotions and paint our own interpretations of hope, faith, charity, sympathy, reverence, ambition, and so forth. We can also interpret grief, sorrow, hunger, want, all of which have prompted great art in the past.

We can take human occupations and glorify them—the man in the field, the miner, the steel builder—anything, almost, that comes to mind. The artist, not the subject, creates the art. Let no artist ever say that he has nothing to paint. Let him strive to develop his understanding of light, form, color, and arrangement so that he can paint absolutely anything. This is not as difficult as it sounds, for all things are simply diverse forms in light and atmosphere, to be studied, arranged, and put into pictures. The artist who cannot paint life may turn to color and design. So many modern paintings are really nothing more than pleasing patterns of color and texture.

Perhaps the art which appeals most to most people is that which conveys emotion of one kind or another. This does not mean that we must always show people doing something emotional. There can be emotion or mood in any painting. A landscape may carry the mood of the surroundings, the mood of the day, like fresh sparkling sunshine, or twilight and stillness. It may be a stream singing over the rocks, a peaceful pasture,

Elephants by Russell Cowles, KRAUSHAAR GALLERIES, NEW YORK CITY.
Animals have their place in art

Other themes can be taken from various human activities, such as sports

Summer by John Koch, KRAUSHAAR GALLERIES, NEW YORK CITY.

Tile Roof by Charles Burchfield, FRANK K. M. REHN GALLERY, NEW YORK CITY

Old barns, quaint houses, factories can all be worthy subjects

City Interior 1936 by Charles Sheeler, WORCESTER ART MUSEUM,
WORCESTER, MASS.

the glory of the sunset, or long shadows cast over white snow. It can be the hot and dazzling brilliance of the desert, the fury of the surf, a lazy stream rippling in a gentle breeze. There are flowers to brighten a wall, birds in gorgeous plumage, villages nestled in the valleys. Getting into the spirit is finding the emotions in a subject, and trying to set them down with paint on canvas. This is something you alone can feel and do and no one else can tell you how. But the emotion becomes the motivating force behind your effort and this will show in the painting, provided you do not bog down in technical difficulties.

Beauty is really an emotional force, and if we find technical means to express it, such emotion will be felt. Beauty is so broad in its scope that it would be hard to miss it entirely if we tried. There is beauty in vigor and force, and there is tranquil beauty. There is voluptuous beauty, bizarre beauty, dignified beauty, serene beauty. There is beauty in basic form, in planes, and in textures. There is beauty in animated form, in classic form. There is beauty in the elements, the minerals, in all inanimate form. We are given such an abundance of beauty that we take it for granted, and unless we focus upon it, we are not even conscious of it. We might say that a man could not move ten feet without seeing some kind of beauty, provided he has the eyes to see it.

Even if this world had been but a barren desert, there still would have been beauty. A friend of mine paints nothing but the desert. To him there is enough beauty there to paint for the rest of his life. The beauty he finds is almost his religion, and his heart is as young as it ever was.

With a world so full of it, how can we ever feel that there is nothing to paint?

There is a big difference between "pretty art" and beautiful art. Pretty art is usually not profound, not truly studied or true to the beauty of nature. It usually consists of pretty colors assembled as in a piece of embroidery, or a design on wallpaper. We find "pretty" postcards that have been doctored up in the engraving plant, pretty

pictures in children's books. They serve their purpose. Many prints are framed and sold and make pretty pictures in the home and cottage, but they do not belong in the category of art. To be profound—and beautiful—a work of art must be based on truth with little, if any, compromise.

It is obvious that the artist must manage to surround himself with the kind of beauty that inspires him most. If you live in the United States, no matter in what part, you are not far from sources of enough natural beauty to keep any artist busy for a lifetime.

In the East there is the beautiful and varied Atlantic coast. There are the mountains of New York State and northern New England, with their streams and forests, where the changing seasons are so much more dramatically contrasted that they are in the Far West. There are weather-beaten farmhouses and picturesque historic villages.

In the center of the country the landscape is not so varied, and there is less sense of the past, but the rolling farmlands and changing crops have color and character. Go north and you find the lakes, dunes, and timberlands. Go south and there are fine old plantation houses and tropical gardens, more wooded mountains, and the strange fascination of the swamplands.

In the West much of the ruggedness of the frontier survives in ghost towns, mines, and ranches. The deserts have their own beauty, and so do the tremendous mountain ranges and the magnificent views found along the coast.

All this beauty need not be abandoned for a so-called more sophisticated art. It can still be the basis of art, modern or otherwise, depending upon what the artists of our country make of it. Let us never fall into the error of believing that art can be put into a single category, that it must be this or must be that. The galleries which are at present still only sympathetic to objective art should not close their doors to the non-objective, nor should the modern directors discount everything but the abstract. One brand of art can no

The Outpost by William Thon, MIDTOWN GALLERIES, NEW YORK CITY

Trouble Ahead by Margery Ryerson, NATIONAL ACADEMY OF DESIGN, NEW YORK CITY
There can be emotion or mood in any painting

Quiet Evening by Hobson Pittman, WALKER GALLERIES, NEW YORK CITY

A landscape may carry the mood of the surroundings, the mood of the day

Winter in the Catskills by Doris Lee, WALKER GALLERIES, NEW YORK CITY

Lilacs by Ernest Fiene.   There
are flowers to brighten a wall,
birds in gorgeous plumage, villages nestled in the valleys

more be rationed out to the public to the exclusion of all others than can one brand of coffee or cigarettes or one kind of food.

Art itself is bigger than any artist, art dealer, museum director, or critic. In art the job is always bigger than the man. Few things have ever been done that could not have been done just a little better, and possibly by the very same artist, if he had a longer life in which to develop his talents. Anyone who believes that the utmost has been reached in art is evidencing the first signs of stagnation. Art can never stand still nor reach a state where there is no more to be done. True beauty never becomes obsolete; it may suffer under the tides of fashion, be torn down and buried for ages, but only to be rediscovered and revived again. The reason for this is that the beauty lies in the mind of man.

III. UNITY

Unity in a painting is an intangible quality. While it is difficult to set down a procedure for attaining it, an approach can nevertheless be suggested. Each picture presents a special problem in this respect, but the initial conception of the subject is always important.

It is obvious that the unity must begin with the design and pattern, to bring about a relationship and balance of the areas of the picture. Such balance is affected both by the distribution of values—the lights, middle tones, and darks—and by the placement and amount of area of each in relation to the whole design.

A light area can be brought into relationship with a dark area in two ways, first by contrast, and second by means of intermediate values between the light and the dark. Through such manipulation we form the masses and design of the subject. Nature does a great deal toward setting up these relationships before us, but nature presents us with too wide an expanse all at once. And there is no assurance that when a bit of the whole panorama is enclosed within a rectangle or frame, the patterns within that particular area will be in balance and in good design or arrangement. The artist must create such balance and design within his subject. This is why we cannot hope to produce good design without conscious effort in this direction. It is the reason why we can seldom reproduce nature exactly as we find it.

Of first importance is the necessity of training the eye to see masses flatly and more or less unbroken. That means we must save until later the variations of values within the mass, the highlights and accents of dark, adding them only after we have established a good design of flat pattern. Then as we break this down into planes, color, and detail, we can keep the basic design in mind and not allow it to escape us. By approaching the design this way, you will be surprised at times to find how little must be added to the flat patterns to bring about a third-dimensional feeling or an appearance of receding into space. This can often be done by color without much change of value within the pattern.

This is especially true of the middle ground and distance in a landscape. The foreground carries most of the detail and accentuation, and as the material recedes, it becomes simpler, softer and hazier.

Perhaps the best way to begin in the study of composition and pattern is by painting still lifes. Here we are not so much concerned with space and depth, and can concentrate on the immediate study of pattern. For use in still-life experiments, the artist should have several heavy curtains. The color of these is a matter of choice but one should be of dark value though not black, another of a low middle tone, a third of lighter middle tone, and a fourth of a light tone but not white. Two should be used at a time, one as a ground and the other as a background.

For light objects, a dark background is the logical choice, and for dark objects a light color provides the necessary contrast. With a middle-

Black Lace Parasol by Morris Kantor, PHILLIPS MEMORIAL GALLERY, WASHINGTON, D. C.   Perhaps the best way to begin in the study of composition and pattern is by painting still lifes

toned background, both light and dark objects may be used. Subjects whose values are close together may be set up against either a light or dark background. Experiment with both, and also with different colors until the most suitable pattern, tone, and color relationship is established with the objects at hand.

The reason neither black nor white is desirable for curtains is that some reserve should be kept for the highlights or dark accents within the subject.

Since the unity of a subject is of prime importance, let us talk for a moment about unity of line. Every picture, though not always obviously, is basically composed of line. All lines in a subject bear a relationship to one another in the way they are placed in the composition and also in the mood they convey. Horizontal lines are associated with tranquillity, vertical lines with growth, diagonal lines with drama, and curves with graceful movement. The greater the curves the more energy and motion are expressed. Subjects may range from peaceful or restful ones all the way to those of violent action according to the kind of line used and how lightly or boldly it is drawn. Here lies a way to unlimited variety.

Such line either may be felt beneath the masses or the movement of the masses, or may be in actual contours within the masses or their edges. The boundaries of any form on a flat canvas produce either stability or some kind of movement. The eye follows line, any line, straight or curved, and it will stop at any crossing of straight lines or merging of lines into a point. Lines radiating from a point lead the eye to that point, and this can be a very valuable device for establishing the focal point, or point of interest, that every composition should possess.

In nature we so often find unity in values, one perfectly related to another, that for the most part values can be accepted as they are, so long as we are able to reach them in our pigmentary range. This is not so true of line. We can of course accept the contours of living forms, but

even these may have to be arranged to fit into a rhythmic pattern. People may be posed for graceful and rhythmic line. Animals may be so placed in the arrangement or design that they become a part of it. The contours of land and those of trees and other growing things may be set into design.

Any design is more effective when the half-tones within the design are minimized and the larger and flatter areas of tone take their place among other simple tones. For power and simplicity the large flat tones are best. The more contrast, the more intense and dramatic effect. The closer in values the masses are painted, the more reserved and quiet the subject will be. There is quiet unity and forceful unity. Close values permit more variety of shape and contour, without upsetting and destroying unity, than strongly contrasting values do. But it is safe to say that the stronger the contrasts in a subject, the simpler its patterns should be.

The same can be said of color. When colors are close in value a wide range of colors may be used with beautiful effect. But huge patches of contrasting color may easily become garish and overpowering. One way of achieving unity with colors is to mix a little of one color throughout all the colors of the subject.

To find the color values of your masses it is best to experiment with shades of color on your palette, or on a separate piece of board, before you actually start to paint. This will show you the range of values at your disposal. If you are painting outdoors the chances are that you cannot reach the whole range you see before you. You then decide whether you wish to sacrifice the values at the top or those at the bottom of your scale. But bear in mind that the light values in your picture make the picture. People generally do not like dark and dreary paintings. It has always seemed to me personally that low values will not be missed as much as the bright ones. In portraits, if you have to paint some values lower than they appear to the eye in order to maintain the brilliancy of your lights, this does not matter

William Rush Carving Allegorical Figure of the Schuylkill River (Final Version) by Thomas Eakins, PHILA-DELPHIA MUSEUM OF ART, PHILADELPHIA.   People may be posed for graceful and rhythmic line

In portraits, if you have to paint some values lower than they appear to the eye in order to maintain the brilliancy of your lights, this does not matter . . . so long as you have achieved brilliancy where it belongs

Portrait Study by Raphael Soyer, ASSOCIATED AMERICAN ARTISTS, NEW YORK CITY.

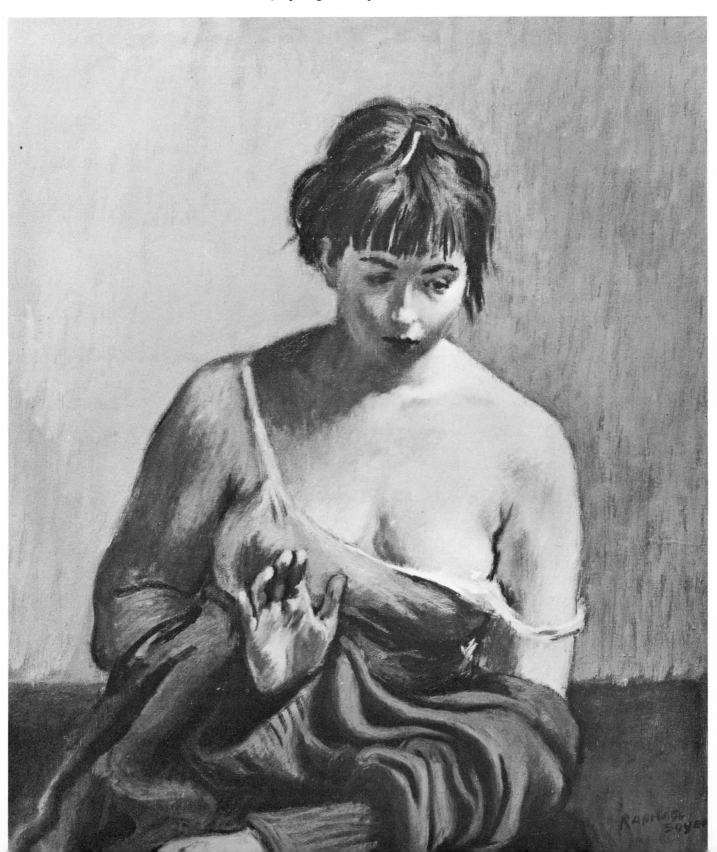

too much, so long as you have achieved brilliancy where it belongs. Outdoors perhaps the reverse is true. An over-all lightness and airiness in your subject may cause you to lose a little of the brilliance of the sky by contrast, but it keeps you from making the kind of heavy, dark paintings which were so common during the eighties and nineties, and which are for the most part now resting—face to the wall—in the storage rooms of museums. It was to get away from this type of picture that Monet, Pissarro, and Van Gogh turned to the high-keyed impression.

There is a great deal more latitude in respect to values in still life than in landscape. Still life may be painted in a higher or lower key to good effect either way. This is simply like raising or lowering the curtain of your studio window, or seeing more or less light on your subject. In fact, you might start a still life on a dark or cloudy day and pick it up again on a brighter day to find all the light areas raised in value, while the dark objects or areas seem even darker. That is simply because light increases contrast between lights and darks. Darkness draws them closer and closer together until all is dark. Twilight is a good critic of your canvas. If the patterns and design hold up in twilight you may be sure they will in good light.

Consistency is another important element in the unity of a design. Whether your subject is objective or abstract, to make a good painting it must have consistency. Realism should at least be plausible. This sort of consistency always seems to exist in nature. For instance, during the seasons, there is a consistency of form, color, and texture that quickly identifies the season. When the leaves turn in color during the fall, the ground has undergone a change also. The bright green of the grass is gone with the green of the foliage. Reds, browns, and low-toned yellows appear on the ground along with the fallen leaves. And because these leaves have changed to warm colors, the mountains which looked blue in the summer now appear purple, for the blue atmosphere

cannot absorb the red as it did the green. Because it is shining on more warm color, the sunlight itself seems more golden in the fall.

The colors of winter are consistent in their drabness, even when they appear in sharp contrast to brilliant blue skies and glistening snow.

In the spring color starts coming to life. The drab colors of winter become interspersed with bright new color. The budding trees take on more red; the new grasses and mosses become brilliant and the dark, wet ground offers greater contrast with the sky.

Midsummer usually sends the artist to the seacoast or to find subjects other than the pastoral landscape, for when all is green the play of color is lacking. He seeks the cottages, the mills, the barns, the stables, rather than the fields and the woods. He finds streams, docks with boats and their reflections, rocks and surf—subjects with color and action. Or else he may paint still lifes and flowers or occupy himself with portraits and figure studies.

It takes an observing eye to recognize the consistency that is so vital to a picture. In this connection I would like to call attention to the work of Andrew Wyeth, who is still a young man and one of the most popular American painters of today. His work is popular not only with the public but with artists and the most exacting critics. It is steeped in the interest of observation and is consistently good all the way down to the last carefully arranged detail. Wyeth finds drama and excitement in ordinary things, proving that if the artist has enough insight he need not go far to find a subject.

In the matter of lighting, consistency means that light from the same source pervades the subject, and each value is related to it. In nature everything seems to be just where it belongs in its scale of values, and unless the artist takes his cue from what nature teaches, his values are likely to appear jumpy and his colors dead. Consistency of light pertains not only to value, but to direction. The direction of the light source will de-

Seed Corn by Andrew Wyeth, KNOEDLER GALLERIES, NEW YORK CITY.
It takes an observing eye to recognize the consistency that is so vital
to a picture

termine which planes can be in full light, which in half-light, and which in shadow. Failure to recognize this principle has cost many an artist the difference between a brilliant and mediocre piece of work.

If there is more than one light source, the problem is that much more difficult, since two general sets of values must be considered. When there are more than two light sources, the artist is almost certain to get lost, and had better either wait until the light situation changes or select another area or subject to paint.

If we have brilliant light, the reflected light will usually take care of overly dark shadows. Reflected light in a painting can be infinitely more beautiful than direct light. It has a way of bringing out form, especially in contrast to the more flatly lighted bright planes.

If we recognize the qualities of direct and indirect light and translate these accurately onto canvas, our painting should have unity. We may say that if the light is right the values are right and the picture will be given unity by the light and values. Light establishes texture, and color too. If the light is right but the picture persists in being bad, then the fault must rather be in the design, the drawing, or the pattern.

Every painting should display a consistency of style. Abstract painting should be consistently abstract, and realism should be consistently true to life. Though there may be exceptions, I question whether these two approaches—or any other ones—can be mixed satisfactorily in a single painting.

If a picture has an idea, let the whole picture be consistent with that idea. However, to avoid monotony—and the completely orthodox picture can be trite and very ordinary—liberties may be taken to give greater pictorial interest. Planned contrasts have value. In a still life, an exquisite piece of jewelry combined with some faded and worn slippers might stir the viewer's imagination. But it would be altogether too inconsistent to paint a portrait of a woman wearing such jewelry and sitting on a stool peeling potatoes.

Lack of consistency in design will detract from beauty. As stated above, abstract forms belong with other abstract forms, realism with realistic forms. Where realism has been reduced to the abstract, then all the realism of the subject should be treated likewise. Realistic hands growing out of inanimate material can be little more than glorified cartooning.

From the mental or emotional side, consistency is plain good taste and common sense. There is nothing to stop anyone from doing the ridiculous, and if he does so he naturally does so on his own. We all have the same privilege.

Another kind of consistency relates to the treatment of a subject. Flatness of treatment is one approach, and the round or modeled another, and the two do not seem to belong together, though we see many paintings in which such an attempt has been made. We see rounded figures emerging from flat planes, like heads poking through a piece of cardboard, bodies emerging from stone walls, or modeled clouds rising above buildings that have no third dimension. I have seen round smoke coming out of a perfectly flat locomotive, round heads rising above perfectly flat costumes and bodies. This seems hardly a matter of artistic license, but plain inconsistency. Were the heads also painted flat, as in early Egyptian art, there would be some logic in the whole.

It is frequently to be observed that pictures when painted toward the flat gain something by having a better relationship to the flat canvas than those which are excessively modeled in the round. For the same reason, in architecture bas reliefs usually have more beauty than completely rounded sculpture, because they are more appropriate to the flat planes of the building. Only when a sculptured figure is separated from the flat plane, as a memorial figure on a pedestal, does it seem to call for the complete third dimension.

There is always the danger that a subject may be so rigidly designed that it becomes static. Here is where one or more accidental effects can provide pleasing contrast. Accidental-looking effects can also, in reality, be planned. They can be achieved technically by not finishing every part of a picture completely. Just as a sculptor often leaves traces of his chisel in places, especially in garments or drapery where the lack of finish adds rather than detracts, so the painter can do the same kind of thing with his brush. In a portrait, the garment may not be as finished as the head; in a still life one or two flowers may carry much more detail and finish than the rest, or the drapery behind objects may be less completely painted than the objects themselves. Planned contrasts thus have a very important place in painting and need not detract at all from the unity of a picture.

An instructor once told me that a picture should suggest that the painting was stopped while the painter was still having a good time. This is difficult, as we all have a natural tendency to carry the finish to the last fingernail or pebble on the ground. When the value within an area is correct, and the color harmony is there, we can be a little brutal with the form, before it gets to the point where it vies with everything else for finish. In order to have form that we can leave unfinished, we must approach the form simply at first and in simple planes, and work all over the subject, bringing it to completion simultaneously rather than piecemeal. Finishing one part at a time more or less excludes the possibility of a spontaneous and lively-looking picture. If we can, we must think of the whole picture all the time, and of every part as it fits into the whole design.

IV. SIMPLICITY AND HOW TO ACHIEVE IT

Our aim for simplicity and clarity must logically start with the subject itself. In choosing our subject we should first consider how effective it would be in a small sketch, say no larger than 5 by 7 inches. Could the material be set down in a sketch of that size? Could it be done without using a very fine brush or would some of the important details be too small? If it is impossible to make a small sketch without infinite labor, then we can be pretty sure we are starting off on the wrong foot. It is safe to say that any subject that will look effective in an exhibition gallery or on the wall of an average-sized living room is also definable in a 5-by-7-inch sketch at a distance of 6 feet or more.

Even though in a small sketch we would normally only suggest the outlines and forms of a subject, the patterns should be simple enough to make the design carry ten feet or more. If the small sketch will do that we may be sure the larger canvas will be effective under any circumstances. This is a very good reason for making a small statement of any subject before we invest effort in a larger one.

Assuming that you usually do most of your oil painting indoors, you will need sketches of outdoor scenes for reference. Make a small sketch for color alone. This, coupled with pencil sketches for detail, or photographs of the spot, will provide much better source material for the final work than will an attempt to make a larger and detailed preliminary painting in the limited time at your disposal outdoors. If your sketch box is large, try using large brushes. Concentrate on color, tone, and pattern. Leave the detail for pencil and camera.

The writer has learned by experience that the artist has not much more than one hour to set down his subject before the light begins to change. If you try to paint too long and then have to go back over your sketch to "warm it up," because it looks too cold in the later light, the original color relationships will be thrown out of balance and the sketch will become progressively worse and inaccurate.

Since we are going to have to simplify most subjects anyway in the finished work, it is better to start eliminating in the sketch. If you take photographs for reference you can always put back a detail here or there in the final composition, should it seem to require it.

Sometimes a subject improves in the warmer light of late afternoon. In this case don't try to work over your original colors; start again or take some color shots. The point is not to mix two separate color versions in your final painting. Choose one or the other and stick to it. The one-o'clock lighting and color will never fit a five-o'clock version. If you are seeking late-afternoon effects, we can sometimes extend your time limit for the sketch by starting out a little earlier and purposely making your colors a little warmer than they appear. However, this takes considerable experience and skill, especially as allowance should also be made for lengthening shadows. Just as colors change, so do shadows, as the afternoon wears on.

We can save ourselves a good deal of trouble

SIMPLICITY AND HOW TO ACHIEVE IT

by selecting simple subjects for our paintings. Scenes involving too many trees, rocks, mountains, people, animals, buildings, clouds, or whatever, can become complicated unless many are eliminated or minimized. Even if a very full scene appeals to you, it is a good idea to see if it is possible to group some of the units into simple patterns. For instance, thousands of trees on a mountainside might be so grouped that they could be suggested in two or three patterns and painted with comparatively few strokes of a dry brush. There are many such possibilities.

The more complicated and intricate the patterns, the larger the area of canvas you should use to accommodate your subject comfortably. Busy patterns can be contrasted with simple patterns with good effect, but a picture that is busy all over will always suffer in comparison to a picture of simple and dramatic design.

As mentioned before, the artist should choose either to simplify what he sees or to select a simpler subject. Or he might choose to paint part of what he sees rather than the whole subject. For example, he may select a barn rather than the whole farm, or even a part of the barn with an animal or two in front of it. Most amateur painters try to include too much, while the experienced painter knowingly focuses his attention on the most interesting part of the scene before him.

Painting is very much like writing. There can be so many detailed passages in a book that the reader who wants the story to move along becomes irritated. A conversationalist can get lost in detail and trivia too, and so can the artist.

It is in massing and grouping (in creating design which did not exist before) that the artist can outdo the best results of color photography. If realistic or objective art is to continue, it will be largely because of this sort of creativeness. The camera has already supplanted the kind of painting which is a slavish copy of nature, and it is left to the artist to paint the essence of what he sees, rather than the frozen exterior image. He must take his subject apart. He must find out

what gives it life, why it is of interest to him, why he wants to paint it. If the design or natural pattern of a subject interests him most, let him stress that, or if it is chiefly the color that thrills him, let that continue to be his main inspiration. Sometimes a subject presents a fascinating design, a happy combination of architecture, or a rhythmic grouping of figures, perhaps, yet the colors are drab. Here the artist can utilize the shapes he wants and add brilliance through broken or stepped-up color. He thus tries to put good color with good design.

Taking a subject apart is rather like taking apart a machine whose performance is sluggish or otherwise less than satisfactory. If some parts do not function well we replace them with new parts; we clean out the dirt and put everything back together so the machine operates more effectively. It would be hard to find a subject in nature where nothing detracts, and nothing needs to be eliminated. In breaking down his subject the artist must decide upon essentials, the things that really make the subject effective, and he must weed out or minimize the rest.

The creative process is brought into play when the artist looks at a subject and decides how to make a good picture out of it. He does this in much the same way that he would if he were looking at a painting by another artist, asking himself how it could be improved if it were to be repainted. He translates what he sees into his own creative terms. Approaching nature in this manner, he may say to himself, here is a chance for rich contrasts, or here is a subject that calls for a very high, delicate key. And he will usually think of the subject in terms of his own particular technique—one subject suggesting, possibly, a strongly built underpainting, another a subtle juxtaposition of colors or forms. Who knows precisely what the artist's thoughts are? But we do know that a sense of exhilaration comes over all of us in anticipation of creating a work of art.

More often than not, the final painting fails

Danger by Thomas Benton, ASSOCIATED AMERICAN ARTISTS, NEW YORK CITY. In breaking down his subject the artist must decide upon essentials, the things that really make the subject effective, and he must weed out or minimize the rest

to come off as well as the artist had anticipated. This may be so because at the time of the initial visualization there is a minimum of thought about the thousand and one things that usually happen once the execution has begun. While he concentrates on true values, on color or form, somewhere down the line, some of the effects an artist may have hoped for will have been lost. His first look at the scene he wants to paint reveals unity and beauty, with all things as they should be. The execution is simply a statement of ability and comprehension. One process is completely visual, the other completely technical. No man's technical ability can ever quite reach the whole truth, even as *he* as an individual may see it.

We must also realize that in our first appraisal of a scene we usually look at the whole and are moved by it. Then later, after our work starts, we may notice the little things we overlooked and gradually, by concentrating on these increasingly bothersome details, lose sight of our original impression, the important impression that made us select the subject in the first place. Therein lies the danger of missing the boat. The hand can become heavy and exhilaration turn to increasing disappointment and at times frustration. There is only one antidote. Take a rest and try again. See if you can remember where it was you began to go wrong, at what point you lost the first impression. See if you can leave out everything that interfered with your first great sweep of vision. Eliminate all but what you think must be in the picture to make it dramatic and intelligible. If your subject was a building, you might not have noticed at first just how many little windows there were. To avoid a busy or crowded look, you might paint these windows, or some of them, very close in value to the main value of the building itself. Or if your scene encompassed a large area of water, you might improve it the second time by eliminating many of the little wavelets and by concentrating on the larger patterns. In figure studies, hands are often troublesome, and while you certainly can't eliminate

them, you can sometimes simplify the problem by suggesting fingers in an impressionistic manner, or painting a hand with the fingers closed. Look over your subject for the many little things that you can eliminate to bring you back to a larger, simpler composition.

Our power of analysis can only come by degrees. It cannot develop from rule and formula alone. This may be helpful, but it is really intelligence dictated by taste and experience that helps us most. We can study for a while with a teacher, but in actual fact there is not a teacher in the world that is not limited to his own viewpoint and ability. Art is stressed in schools today, and there are many special art schools and summer classes for amateurs and budding professionals. But the question is: How much creativeness can be taught? This is something that is either inborn or developed by the unflagging interest, study, and hard work of the individual himself.

Besides cutting down the amount of material in a picture for the sake of simplification, we should of course also look, and look well, at the material we do put in. We find among artists, especially artists with commercial experience, a tendency to round out and finish every part of the subject so that equal importance is given to everything. This means that no part of the subject has been subordinated and too many elements compete for attention. It is almost imperative that the artist search for a key motif and stress it.

All paintings should have a focal point. This will be the object or group of objects that you feel is of most importance to your theme and your design. Concentrate your sharpest detail or color here, and subordinate it elsewhere. If other spots are too insistent, eliminate some of the highlights and accents, bring the values closer, fuse the edges, or lessen the competing brilliancy of color.

An important means of simplification is to see your patterns or areas of tone as flatly as possible. They should not be broken up or overmodeled with too many obvious planes. Think of light as

Breezing Up by Winslow Homer, NATIONAL GALLERY OF ART, WASH-
INGTON, D. C.   All paintings should have a focal point. This will be
the object or group of objects that you feel is of most importance to
your theme and your design

Young Woman by Isabel Bishop, MIDTOWN GALLERIES, NEW YORK CITY. In figure studies, hands are often troublesome, and while you certainly can't eliminate them, you can sometimes simplify the problem by suggesting fingers in an impressionistic manner, or painting a hand with the fingers closed

one plane, halftone as another, and shadow as a third, painted simply and almost flat. I do not mean that the planes should get "tinny" and perfectly smooth. There can, and should, be variation of color. But if you think of the whole light as opposed to the whole shadow, with the intervening halftone as a means of uniting the two, your picture will be simpler and, as a rule, more effective.

The importance of flatness and simplicity is emphasized in the carrying power of a poster. While a painting should not look like a poster, there is, nevertheless, a lesson to be learned here. So often a painting suffers by the presence of too many subtle values throughout the value scale. With little separation of pattern and little empha-

sis on design a picture looks weak from a distance. There may well be delicacies within the patterns, the change of values may be subtle, but the design should embrace these subtleties within the stronger patterns. Perhaps no painter used more subtle values than Corot, but an examination of his paintings shows that he held his pattern and design; in fact his work seems always to be based upon design.

Degas was a great master of pattern, color, and design. His pastels are patterns of broken color, with the patterns lying nearly flat, though full of different colors which are close in value. He did not hesitate to let a figure disappear under the frame if that helped the design.

Howard Pyle was one of the first American

Rehearsal on the Stage by Edgar Degas, METROPOLITAN MUSEUM OF ART, NEW YORK CITY.   Degas was a great master of pattern, color, and design. . . . He did not hesitate to let a figure disappear under the frame if that helped the design

illustrators to realize the true pictorial value of organized pattern. If we study his work, we note that he gave great consideration to keeping lights, middle tones, and darks generally separated into large areas of each. In some pictures he built his lights and darks into a general overtone of gray; in others he put his middle tones and lights into a dominant field of dark. With four general values he shows us the following combinations:

(1) halftones and darks against light
(2) lights and darks against light gray
(3) lights, darks and light grays against dark gray
(4) lights and grays against dark

This is the key to pattern-making in pictures. Whole areas may be enveloped in shadow for the dark pattern or left very light to produce patterns in a high key. In a landscape, the foreground might be in shadow and the distance in light. Or the reverse might be true. Cloud shadows or cast shadows on the ground can produce interesting patterns, and so, at the other end of the scale, can rays of direct or reflected light.

We can use busy patterns with simple ones in the same picture. But never should all our patterns be the same. Suppose you have decided to paint a stream bed filled with rocks, and then you find there are mountains above it with equally broken up and busy formations, and above these mountains a sky broken up with many small clouds. One or more of these areas will need simplification in the painting. If the river bed is your main interest, concentrate detail here and keep the mountains and the sky areas relatively free of conflicting patterns. You might even omit the clouds entirely for a better measure of contrast. Nature provides copious material for our selection. We cannot effectively duplicate everything exactly as we see it; therefore it is in our selection, first, in our ability to scale down and organize contrasting areas of pattern into a harmonious composition, second, and in our technical skill with pencil or brush, third, that our stature as an artist is weighed.

After considering the pattern areas of your subject, next think about the planes. These are the lines which characterize each object and make it recognizable. They should be kept as simple as possible. Like the sculptor, the painter eliminates unnecessary line. He may flatten his forms, work for masses, strive for rhythmic relationships, even distort where distortion enhances his idea.

If a surface has many small and complicated planes an attempt should be made to reduce them to fewer and larger ones. A woman's dress looks better after it has been ironed—when little wrinkles have been smoothed out and when the material falls in fewer and more flattering folds. The result is more beautiful because the simplicity of line has been restored. If we paint a dress and add so much detail that it begins to look messy and in need of ironing, the painting will fail in its attempt to be beautiful. A dress should be neither painted like sheet metal nor overmodeled. And the same principle holds for other subjects. Find enough planes to define the form, then stop before the area gets messy.

Even a head may be reduced to larger planes without loss of form. Just as you try to find the underlying design of drapery as it hangs in folds, watch for the same sort of pattern in hair. Connect the planes of light, halftone, and shadow. Then put in only as many smaller planes within these areas as you need to suggest the character of hair. The shadows will stand more simplification than the lights, for detail and textures belong to the light, while shadows are more obscure and opaque. Muddiness in a picture most often results from too many and too dark halftones in the lighted areas.

Much can be done in the way of simplification by the handling of edges. Too many sharply defined edges confuse a subject with patterns and reduce the picture's carrying power. They cut up the material into small bits, where masses are called for. The "lost and found" edges of objects —against a light or dark background—unify the whole picture, and the artist's job is to pull these together, to blend and interlace and modify patterns that would otherwise remain hard and separate.

Finally, simplification can be achieved by reducing the number of values used. The picture with three or four main values or masses will be simpler and more effective than one with many values. It is possible to produce fifteen to twenty slight variations of value between black and white. But a few feet away these values will merge into what seems an unseparated gradation of tone from white to black. The same thing happens to a picture in which the values are not more widely separated. This, of course, practically eliminates pattern and design.

The best working plan is to use about eight values, with a division of two values to a pattern. While this would mean using four patterns, it does not necessarily mean dividing a picture up into four separate areas, as the patterns may interweave or be broken up in any way the composition may require. Furthermore, some of the patterns may well be separated more by the difference of color than by value. The possibilities of design, using even a limited range of colors and values, are almost limitless.

Arrangement and design are more easily controlled in portraits and still lifes than in any other types of paintings. In portraits, the artist can design his subject as he sets it up, placing his patterns of lights, middle tones, and darks as he wishes, through arrangement of costume, background, and accessories. For example, knowing that he will be painting a subject in a white satin dress, he can choose either a middle or a dark tone for the background. And the actual costume and head of the sitter may provide enough design in itself for the elimination of all other patterns. With still life the problem is even easier, for the artist can select anything he likes from a world full of material and arrange his objects and colors at will.

V. DESIGN

Design may mean the presentation and expression of form itself, such as in sculpture, or of some sort of flat ornamentation applied to form, such as in a surface decoration, or it may refer to the particular arrangement of objects in a painting where shading and the principles of perspective have been employed to give them a life-like, three-dimensional quality.

Since in painting our aim is to represent three-dimensional objects on a flat surface, it is this type of design that concerns us here. We shall leave solid design to the fields of sculpture, ceramics, and other three-dimensional objects. However, no matter how it is used, design involves many of the same elements: simplicity of form, planes, color, texture.

For the moment, let us ignore halftone and shadow as usually associated with the rendering of solid form and consider the elements associated with the flat-design treatment of light and dark areas (chiaroscuro) in a picture.

What is the purpose of our design? Is it intended to be an entity within itself for the sole purpose of creating beauty, or is it to serve as ornament in a larger scheme, such as an interior? The surroundings can sometimes be made to harmonize with a pictorial design, but more often a design is made—or chosen—to accent and embellish the environment. In any event, harmony should exist between the finished design itself and the background upon which it is either hung, or (in the case of a mural) painted directly.

An abstract painting is a logical choice for a modern interior; on the other hand, any well-painted picture is at an advantage when hung on the plain background that most modern and contemporary rooms provide. Few paintings, except the classical type of portrait or flower study, look well against a pattern (wallpaper) background, and most pictures in elaborately ornamented gold frames look correspondingly out of place in a contemporary setting.

The trends in interior decoration are toward light, airy treatments, with simple planes of wall, ceiling, and floor, with splashes of color in textiles, furniture, and accessories. The paintings that suited the dark oak-paneled interiors of the past do not fit a modern interior. Today's realistic paintings, if they are to compete with abstractions as wall decoration, must have more pronounced design, more vivid color, larger pattern, and less halftone and modeling of form.

Contemporary fashions in interior decorating have also swung our taste away from the very ornate rococo type of gilded picture frame and toward simple, or at least simpler moldings textured with gesso. And flat, wide frames are more often the artist's choice than the older narrow and protruding types. Here again, simplicity is the keynote.

Modern art is proving that it takes very little material to make a picture. If a few well-balanced flat color areas can be so effective in an abstract painting, the same can be true of an objective one. The more conservative painter can benefit by studying modern art without prejudice and applying some of the same principles.

What we paint is very important to us, but how

Slumbering Fields by William Palmer, MIDTOWN GALLERIES, NEW YORK CITY.   Modern art is proving that it takes very little material to make a picture. If a few well-balanced flat color areas can be so effective in an abstract painting, the same can be true of an objective one

we paint it and to what purpose is equally important. The treatment of a subject can be even more important than the subject itself. The artist is free to choose the subjects that interest him most—he does not have to paint clowns or fat nudes just because some modern artists do; he does not have to stop painting landscapes or flowers if he likes painting landscapes or flowers, but he may learn new ways of doing it. Studying modern art does not mean copying it any more than the study of Renaissance painting means that a painter intends to reproduce a Titian or a Botticelli. Rather does it mean that by exposing

ourselves to various styles of painting we learn a lesson from each.

Today we might wish we could paint as well as, let us say, Gainsborough, but our concept would be entirely different. Portraits in themselves are by no means passé. It is only the overly formal approach that may at times make them seem so. We live in an era of informality and of speed, and unless our paintings have a light, spontaneous, impressionistic quality, they are likely to seem out of date.

The painters of yesterday used certain patterns and styles that need not be adhered to today. We

East River by Dong Kingman, MIDTOWN GALLERIES, NEW YORK CITY.   What we paint is very important to us, but how we paint it and to what purpose is equally important. The treatment of a subject can be even more important than the subject itself

get to thinking that a woman must be painted in her best low-necked gown, fingering her string of pearls. A more modern approach might be to paint her curled up in an easy chair with a book or magazine, or to paint her arranging flowers, or out walking with her dog, or astride a horse, or doing anything that is characteristic of her. We don't have to imitate Sargent, William L. Chase, or anybody else. Our paintings must be contemporary and as fresh and alive-looking as possible.

What is really needed in fine art is for the artist's conception to be overhauled to fit the times; it is a change in our attitude, rather than a change of subject, that will help us most. And with the change, new techniques may also develop.

When we come to the actual design of a subject, it is easier to enumerate the things we should not do than to try to say precisely what to do, for every artist must develop his own individual style. But there are some simple rules which are more or less obligatory for success:

Shapes and areas of your composition should be varied in form and color and unequal in size. For instance, in an outdoor subject the sky area should not equal the ground area.

Avoid arrangements that split the subject down or across the middle.

Balance large units or spots with smaller ones. A large unit in the foreground can be balanced with a smaller one in the distance.

In realistic painting establish a point of view and an eye-level and stick to it.

In abstract painting, play up color and texture. This is as important as the design itself.

Do not show extremes of proportion, such as a very large head with small figures behind it. It is difficult for the eye—or even the camera—to focus at the same time on an extreme close-up and great distance.

Every good composition gives a route for the eye to follow and strives to hold the eye within the subject as long as possible. This has been called the line of sight, the line of vision, the eye-path, or the leading line. It is an effort to control the viewer's eye, as it travels through the picture. In general, we try to give the eye only one entrance to the picture and one exit from it. It is like choosing a natural path over the terrain as we might do if we were actually walking into such a scene. We begin the path, or line, at the bottom of the picture, and then by the arrangement of other lines, edges, spots, and accents our eye is carried comfortably through the subject, and finally, via a focal point, it finds an exit at the top. Should the eye be blocked near the middle of the composition by some obviously impassable object, it should be directed one way or the other around the object by a logical pathway, by lines or spots, and then be directed upwards again by the placement of smaller obstacles at the other side of the picture. If a tree is the obstacle in question, low bushes or rocks might be added on one side of it, while the other side is left open for the eye to travel into the distance. With a portrait, all lines lead toward the head, on the principle of a focal point with radiating lines. Even a still life can be given a pleasing eyepath by arranging the objects in an attractive sequence.

In abstract art, an eyepath is not so important, since we ordinarily dispense with much depth, and the eye rests upon the whole canvas as a flat plane, as it would on any flat design.

Sometimes the eye may be directed by cast shadows and their edges, by a rut in the ground, by puddles, small streams, bits of deadwood, or patches of bare ground or flowers. It obviously will follow an actual worn pathway—a road or a fence—and through association go directly to a gateway or door. But a pathway may be developed on a stretch of open country, such as a plain or a desert, and even in a marine scene. In the latter there can always be jutting rocks, breaking waves with sea spray, wave shadows, strips of land, birds, boats, and clouds. Never let the eye-path go straight up the middle. If we look along a railroad track the eye goes straight to the horizon and must come all the way back to see what is at the sides. Let the eye wander easily from side to side, gradually getting up into the sky, where it may also, perhaps, wander among an interesting formation of clouds. Avoid anything that would carry the eye out of the picture at the sides. If you have a mountain crest running right to the frame, let a treetop show above it, or soften the edge with a bid of cloud. The eye might be coaxed from such an edge by a bird a little above it, by an overhanging branch at the top of the picture, or by a line of a cloud swinging upward from the mountain crest. Curling smoke is another useful device for this purpose. There can be no absolute rules for such details as these; they are a matter of inventiveness. The main idea—or underlying rule—is to be conscious of creating an eyepath.

Subjects with two very similar objects are best avoided. If we must have two, then one must dominate the other. At no time should there be a sense of divided attention, or of competition, unless such competition actually exists, as in a painting of two prizefighters, two battling armies or animals, or other opposing forces. Even in a painting of two prizefighters, the picture will have more unity if they are shown in a clinch (or one up and one down) than if both are shown stand-

SEARCHING FOR ARRANGEMENTS

Design and pattern are essential to every painting. After selecting a subject, the artist should make experimental sketches, breaking up a rectangle with three or four tones, and manipulate the patterns until a pleasing balance of masses is achieved. This is great fun.

A Stag at Sharkey's by George Bellows, NATIONAL GALLERY OF ART, WASHINGTON, D. C.   Even in a painting of two prizefighters, the picture will have more unity if they are shown in a clinch (or one up and one down) than if both are shown standing with space between them

In abstract art, an eyepath is not so important, since we ordinarily dispense with much depth, and the eye rests upon the whole canvas as a flat plane, as it would on any flat design

Prophetic Plane by Mark Tobey, WILLARD GALLERY, NEW YORK CITY.

Portrait of Albert Wolff, by Jules Bastien-Lepage, E. & A. SILBERMAN GALLERIES, NEW YORK CITY

Never put a head or anything else of importance in the exact center of a picture. Drop it, lift it, or place it to one side . . . and never place head and shoulders so they face the viewer squarely

La Femme à la Perle by Jean Corot, LOUVRE

ing with space between them. Two rounded and abrupt shores on a lake, with their reflections in the water, have been known to look more like two whales bumping noses than two shores on a lake. Double portraits, especially of two men or two women are equally difficult to bring off successfully. A mother and child make a good subject because one dominates the other in size. When you must paint two people, have one standing and the other sitting, or dress one in a dark costume, the other in a light one. Do anything to avoid giving two people or two similar objects equal importance in the painting.

The use of overlapping units is a very good way to create unity of design. It ties the picture together and produces a stronger effect. Almost any number of units can be overlapped or arranged into a few groups for the sake of simplification. This was explained in some detail in the last chapter.

Never put a head or anything else of importance in the exact center of a picture. Drop it, lift it, or place it to one side. Center placement is particularly disturbing and irritating in a portrait. A head so placed is like the center point of a target; the eye is held there almost by force and has difficulty in settling elsewhere. In addition to this it gives the impression that the figure has slipped down and is about to fall out of the frame. Make the spaces around the head unequal in three directions—upward, and to each side.

One more don't. In a portrait, never place head and shoulders so they face the viewer squarely. More often than not, this will make the subject look as if he were facing a firing squad, or posing for a passport picture. While this seems obvious, failure to recognize it accounts for many bad portraits.

I believe a great deal can be accomplished in design if we first try to analyze the feeling that a subject gives us, for in creating a painting both mood and atmosphere are very important. If the subject is serene, we emphasize horizontal lines and quiet, clear color; if it is exciting, we employ sweeping curves, big forms, and contrasting colors. If the subject is one of combat and confusion, then we use bold strokes at opposing angles, spearlike shapes, and a dramatic juxtaposition of colors.

In composition, the "S" line, or reverse curve, is a useful device when sheer beauty is our objective. It is perhaps the most beautiful of all lines, suggesting both grace and rhythmic movement at the same time. It flows in gentle rather than rapid motion. Nothing in art moves as fast as a straight line. Even the line an arrow transcribes in the air as it leads to a target is curved, and an arrow's speed is about the maximum speed the eye can follow. Anything of faster speed, such as a bullet, is too fast.

The modern school is continually talking about emotional impact, but this can also exist in realistic art. Line has mood and emotion; so have shapes, colors, and values, apart from the literal. We are daily affected by these, sometimes consciously, sometimes subconsciously. It is my belief that the gray walls of a prison are punishment in themselves. Man would go mad without sunlight and color. To me, gray is associated with death—the rotting tree trunk and mold; gray is at once all colors mixed together and the absence of all those colors. It is ominous, like a leaden sky and water. Yet gray exists in nature, and as a foil for bright colors there is nothing to equal it. It is the most useful neutralizer and modifier.

Too much of any one color is unattractive, and nature teaches us how to balance one with another. Warm colors are offset by the cool, just as heat is relieved by cold. We only begin to know nature when we begin to understand the balance of growth and erosion, life and death. The greatest beauty in painting comes from this elusive and subtle balance of forces.

Balance in a picture can be emotional as well as structural. This completeness seems most beautiful when contrasted in some way with incompleteness. Power in a composition is greatest when bold lines are contrasted with thin or un-

The Fish Kite by Robert Vickrey, MIDTOWN GALLERIES, NEW YORK CITY.   Detail becomes more interesting when a picture also contains simple, broadly painted areas

finished ones. Color is most effective when brilliance is balanced by quiet colors. Detail becomes more interesting when a picture also contains simple, broadly painted areas. Form is more convincing when there is a sense of underlying structure. And so on.

We must give equally serious attention to character and ways of depicting it. Character should be expressed in the simplest possible terms; otherwise its force will be lost. If superficial detail is needed to portray the character of a subject, then the time required to add such detail is well spent. But if structure is the main theme, then overly detailed surface decoration will tend to detract from rather than add to the main characteristic we wish to portray. The character of an animal

can be conveyed better through the lines of its body, its graceful movement, than by the most exact duplication of its fur or markings. A tree is better represented by its lines of growth, its struggle against the elements, its spacing and proportions, than by emphasis on the outlines of individual leaves or the markings of bark. While such details are essential in the illustration of a field guide book, they hamper the freedom of style necessary in the execution of a painting. Where an illustrator's job is to be photographically correct as to detail, an artist's search for character goes deeper.

Feeling can be expressed better in realistic art than it can in abstract painting, for the latter is largely an intellectual affair. There is a "feel"

81

A tree is better represented by its lines of growth, its struggle against the elements, its spacing and proportions, than by emphasis on the outlines of individual leaves or the markings of bark

Shed in the Swamp by Charles Burchfield, CARNEGIE INSTITUTE, PITTSBURGH.

DESIGN

about everything, even the time of day. Early morning, midday, twilight; in each we find a very different character of light and shadow, tone and color. It is hard to define the point at which our analysis of such things leaves off and our emotional reaction begins. Both enter into the artist's conception. In any event, it is important that the feeling of the subject be conveyed to the viewer. Light and color have much to do with conveying it, design and character still more, and emotion, I think, however we express it, most of all.

It is one thing to copy nature, and quite another to express her in our paintings. By thinking in big terms and by using big masses and planes in a free, uninhibited manner the artist can express himself and the "feel" of things most vividly. Big truths can be obscured by many separate little ones if we allow the unimportant to gain the upper hand. The big truths in a landscape, surely, are that the sun is shining, that the shadows reveal a blue sky overhead, that there is atmosphere between you and that distant tree, that the soil is rich beneath the vegetation, that it is a certain time of day and a certain time of the year. It does not matter how many trees or flowers or blades of grass there are, for their presence, en masse, can only be suggested in a representation of a landscape.

I speak of these things here because composition and design cannot be governed by hard and fast rules. Without inventiveness—a certain amount of it, at least—and without feeling, which also cannot be governed by rules, our efforts are likely to produce an externally factual painting without spirit.

I personally consider design more important than idea or subject. If we think long enough and hard enough, almost any subject can be made into an interesting design. We may create the design by placement, by pattern or value, by line and movement, by tonal key and color. And within the outlines of our design we add the intrinsic character of the thing we are painting.

There has been considerable effort to reduce design to a system of mathematics. There are theories of dynamic symmetry and books on the subject. And while such study can be helpful, there can be no substitute for the deep analysis of nature itself. There we find design based upon purpose and function. Fish move through water, birds through the air, and the design of their bodies is admirably adapted to this purpose. The design of vegetation also results from its way of life.

Once in a life class George Bridgman said to me, "My boy, you have drawn a leg, but you have missed the design of the leg." What he meant was that every part is related in size and position to the function of the leg. The bones are curved and of certain length to function together, and the muscles too are positioned for the most efficient operation. Where the movement requires most strength—such as in the calf of a leg—there is the largest development. This is design.

VI. PROPORTION

Although proportion is related to design, it is a tangible quality which can be measured and confirmed. But there is more to the "creation" of proportion than simple measurement. Actual proportion can be measured with certainty, while creative proportion must be accomplished by individual experiment and taste.

Proportion is usually measured by the simple use of a graph in one form or another. We "scale" proportions one to another as they fall within the graph. Whether the method is simple measurement by eye, or the use of a scaled elevation, as in architectural and mechanical drawing, the same principle is involved.

In measuring three-dimensional forms, we must consider all sides as flat design and then assemble the measurement. A house can be built from flat designs of the floor plan, basement, and roof, coupled with flat designs of the sides or elevations. Perhaps it has not occurred to the artist that he draws in exactly the same way. While he introduces the third dimension by the use of perspective, he is really making a flat drawing of a silhouette as his eye sees it.

To get a drawing in proportion, the artist must establish the middle points of the horizontal and vertical lines and consider the height of the subject in proportion to the width. By outlining the boundaries of his picture and then by dividing the height at the middle with a horizontal line and the width by a similar vertical line, he divides the picture into four quarters. After this he can go on to reduce the object to eighths and smaller fractions to help him reproduce the whole object in proportionate scale.

With a graph laid over or held in front of an object we get the proportionate relationships of all the parts. A graph may be laid out on a piece of glass and used as a finder, to arrive at proportions, or the ordinary type of finder itself may be made to serve a double purpose by gluing threads across the opening at the middle and quarter points of the open rectangle.

Easiest of all, the eye may be trained to find the middle point within any set of contours by looking along a straight edge and marking it. Thus the width can be compared to the height and the middle points of both made to coincide. Some artists measure with the thumbnail held over a brush handle; others make an open square with the fingers, or a rectangle that will fit around the desired contours, and judge the relation of width to height in this manner.

It is fairly easy to visualize a square, and buildings may be visually measured by noting how many squares would fit into the area, or what portion of a square would be required to fit around it.

Another very good method of proportioning is to draw the object the same size you see it, by sighting horizontal lines to the side of the board to take in the height, and vertical lines to the top of the board to take in the width. (See Diagram.)

All these methods are simply a means of arriving at contours. When these are blocked in, we must look carefully again for structure. We start

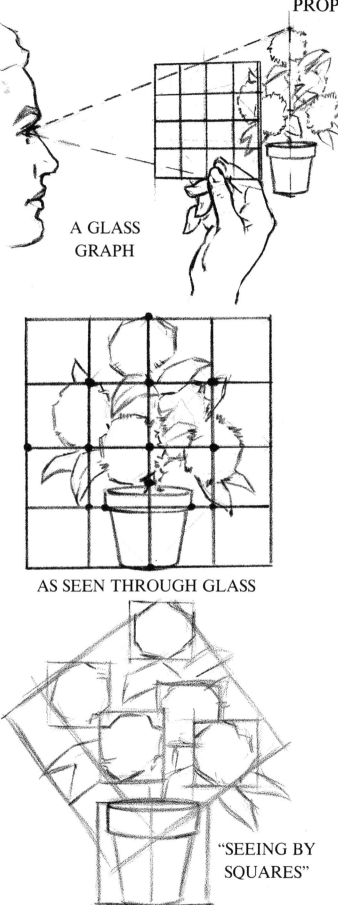

A GLASS GRAPH

AS SEEN THROUGH GLASS

"SEEING BY SQUARES"

FINDING PROPORTION

A square piece of glass ruled in squares with a grease pencil (or eyebrow pencil) is a useful instrument for determining the proportions of a landscape or object. View your subject through the glass—with one eye—and note where the divisions (see dots in center drawing) fall. Spaces between the contours are as important as the contours themselves. As you train your eyes this device will become unnecessary; meanwhile it offers a way of learning to see contours and shapes in relation to one another and to the whole. With this glass you can also check your finished drawing with the actual subject before you.

Also try to learn to see all parts without using a glass. Imagine squares surrounding the main objects of details of the design.

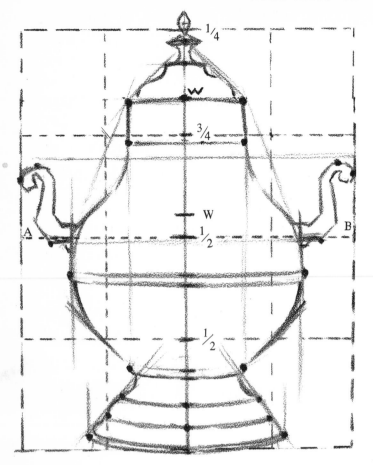

TRAINING THE EYE FOR PROPORTION

Set down two points to indicate height of the object. Measure the width and compare with the height (point W). Indicate the width at half-point of the height (AB). This gives the mid-point of the rectangle which surrounds the object (———). Divide the height and width into fourths (———). Make a mental note of how such dividing lines would appear in front of the object. Now note how the contours would appear in this "mental graph." Try to set down the general shapes in block form within the over-all rectangle. Now look for important points or features that oppose one another on both the horizontal and the vertical planes and note their relationships. Then fill in the contours between these points.

In simple terms you are training your eye to see the rectangle into which the object you are drawing fits. Is it longer, or is it shorter, than a square? Is the height greater or less than the width, and how much? Where is the middle line—up and down or crossways? Where are the quarter-points? What points are opposite? How do they fall beneath each other?

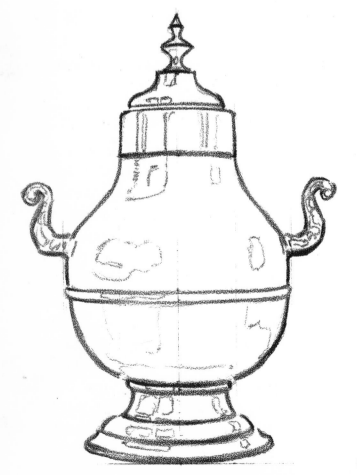

86

with mass alone and then look for form within the contour. In painting there is always the danger of being so much concerned with outline and contour that we do not take in the quality of the form and character of the edges. We are afraid to let go of them as limits of the form, and fail to see that the form merges with other forms.

To return for a moment to the differences between drawing and painting (discussed in an earlier chapter), in drawing we usually see things singly, in outline, while in making a painting we concentrate more on groups of objects and colors, noting what each thing does in the whole effect of the picture. Are there shadows? Do some parts of an object stand out in contrast to the environment? Does a part of the surface form melt into and become closely associated with the shadow? Does part of it seem to disappear altogether? These things are of great concern to us when we paint.

In drawing on a white surface we are naturally concerned with the outlines as they must appear on white, but we cannot transpose these edges to a painting. We must consider what other elements in the painting would affect the object and how. We must be sure of the lighting and its direction, and consider the possibility of the object's giving off or receiving reflected light. Of great importance are the values, which must be consistent with other values, and color, which must be consistent with other color.

When material for a picture is gathered from several different sources and objects are arranged without consideration of basic relationships, there is an obvious lack of unity. We see this often in commercial art. Every student should make a practice of painting subjects which he can set up as a whole, and of studying nature outdoors, where he can see what oneness means and learn how to reproduce it.

In commercial work this is not always possible; nevertheless the man who has experience in painting from life will be equipped to do a much better job of integration. He will be able to paint a properly unified picture instead of making a graphic catalogue of objects within a given area.

In considering proportion in abstract art we face quite a different situation. Here the artist is attempting to do something which cannot be done with realistic proportion.

Suppose he comes upon a scene which he wishes to interpret in an abstract design. Design then is his motif, and he is not interested in proportion, perspective, or the third dimension, but only in form as it contributes to design, and in values without regard to space or their relationship to one another. By eliminating so many of the elements of beauty, he actually gives himself a tougher job than the realistic artist has to face. He is likely to be guided by the things he feels rather than the things he sees.

Van Gogh, whose work is only semi-realistic, must have approached his subjects in this way. It is certain that this Dutch artist sacrificed much to the thing that seemed to enthrall him most—vibrating color. And, like all artists, Van Gogh was much more successful at some times than at others. He maintained enough proportion and drawing to make his subjects recognizable, and his manner of reducing form to images painted in bold, flat strokes results in paintings with a strong decorative quality. It will ever remain a question whether better drawing and proportion would have contributed anything more to his canvases —or, indeed, to the popularity of his work. My own opinion is that with accurate draftsmanship much of his individualism would have been lost.

Accurate proportions alone do not make art; they must be associated with fine value, color, and design. Similarly, inaccurate proportions do not necessarily make bad art. We find paintings in which the drawing is distorted and unacademic and yet the work still qualifies as art. The point is that art is not entirely dependent on drawing.

Some of the great draftsmen were great only as draftsmen, and their paintings added little or nothing to their stature. Dürer was essentially a

THE GRAPH

Nothing has ever excelled the graph as a means of locating contours and points. It is really a two-dimensional procedure superimposed upon a flat image. It can be applied as a mental or actual means of stating graphically the relationship of parts.

Through the invention of a graph that would cover a sphere, man has been enabled to define all the areas of the earth, as well as any spot in an area, by maps.

It becomes a most valuable asset to the artist and draftsman wherever accurate drawing is needed.

The eye can be trained to see a mental graph in front of any object or scene. There is always a middle line and also proportionate divisions that can be used as a guide to accurate rendering.

Almost anyone could draw the accompanying objects by first laying out the proportionate graphs. He could enlarge or reduce the drawing by choice, by simply holding the proportions of the over-all rectangle.

Since it is easy to see any square, all rectangles can be mentally compared to a square and the variation noted. The rectangle can then be divided as needed.

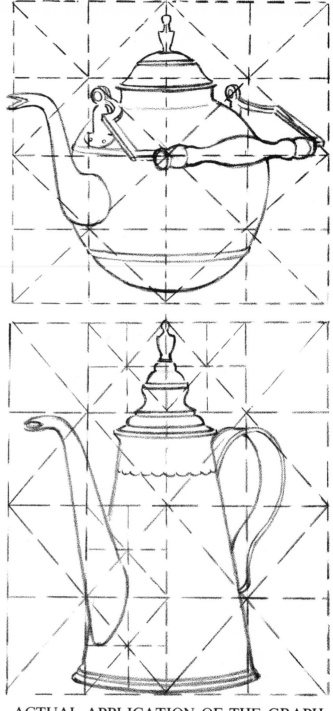

ACTUAL APPLICATION OF THE GRAPH

TO FIND THE
RECTANGLE

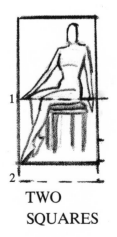

TWO
SQUARES

Suppose we are looking at this tree in real life. We find it fits into a shape that is just a little wider than a square. We look first for point A as the middle point of our design. Then we establish points B,C,D,E as middle points of the sides of the enclosing block, and finally AB, AC,AD,AE, which are the quarter points.

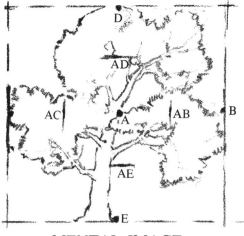

MENTAL IMAGE

Block in the four quarters. Next block in the angles as they fall within the quarters. Now place important points in the contours, in relation to the angles and also to the quarter points. It is easier thus to locate a point in a smaller portion of the object than to guess where it is in relation to the whole object.

This is a method of teaching the eye to measure and to see areas as they are related to each other. Soon you learn to see with amazing accuracy. The eye will automatically look for the enclosing block and big shapes. This is the real secret of successful drawing.

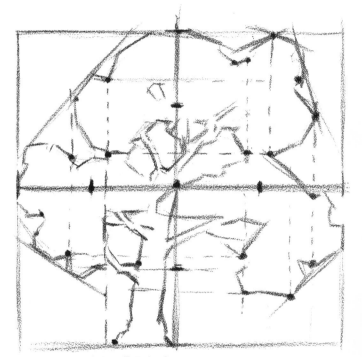

THE DESIGN ON PAPER

The same method applies to any shape. Here a taller and narrower tree has been blocked out in similar fashion.

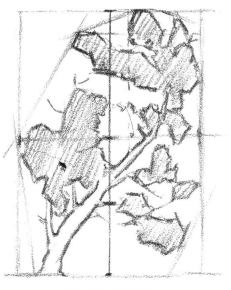

VARIATION

89

TRAINING THE EYE FOR PROPORTIONS

The use of a square also helps greatly in arriving at the proportions of architectural objects. In this drawing it was found that the church nearly fitted into a square. The tower was about one-fourth the width of the square, touching the middle line. The rest of the church fell just under the middle of the square. The tower shows about 3 squares of facing and the roof about 2½ squares, the units of the roof being just a little smaller than the tower units. The smaller buildings were drawn in proportion to the church. The close building was about a square and a quarter high. The width was determined by comparison with the tower, being equal to two squares.

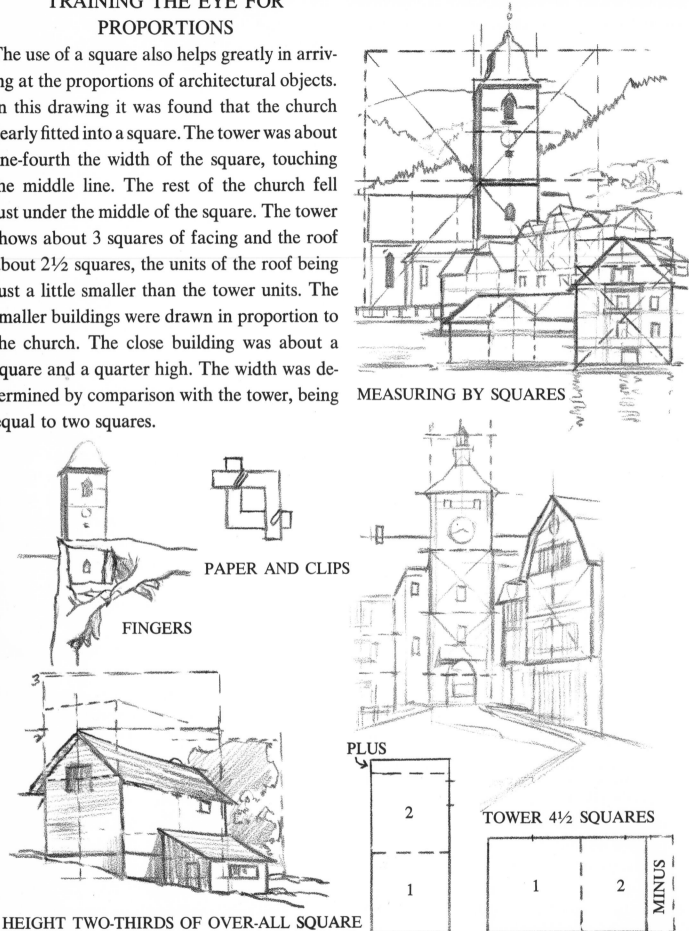

MEASURING BY SQUARES

PAPER AND CLIPS

FINGERS

PLUS

TOWER 4½ SQUARES

2

1

1   2

MINUS

HEIGHT TWO-THIRDS OF OVER-ALL SQUARE

90

draftsman, whereas Van Gogh and the impressionists were great colorists, their drawing having little to do with the success of their work. It is not often that a generation will produce a man who excels in every department of art, or one who produces work having all the combined elements of beauty. Da Vinci was remarkable in this respect, and so of course was Michelangelo, whose paintings and sculptures were equally masterful. When we understand this we can have a great deal more tolerance than most of us have at the start for all art.

We usually find that when a man is stimulated by the love of certain aspects of life, he becomes proficient in presenting these. In the popular field there is the English artist A. J. Munnings, whose paintings of horses have brought him international fame. Munnings became popular not only because of his knowledge of horses but because of his ability to put his horses into a setting with total relationship and understanding, in the same light, with the same good observation throughout the picture. There have been many painters of horses, but I know of none in this century who could paint them and their surroundings quite so well. On the other hand, artists like Degas and Manet, in the last century, made many studies of the racetrack in a far livelier style than Munnings'.

Dufy, in this century, has furthered the impressionist tradition. Modern artists draw for expression and accentuation of poignant faces, and the result can be better than if they stuck entirely to the actual. Their work departs from "photographic" representation. In this respect, it has always been my contention that proportion appears to our two eyes quite differently from the way it appears to the single lens of the camera. Certainly the camera distorts considerably when it is too close to an object.

An excellent way to draw is to make a most careful drawing in as true proportions as possible, then make a second drawing from the first, instead of going back to life. In the second drawing we try to get the essence of the first, taking liberties in the streamlining of the contours, adding blockiness to forms that seem too round, flattening forms to produce more design, changing the proportions if we think we can make them more expressive. Above all, we can eliminate much insignificant detail and stress simplicity.

If you are using a photograph, instead of working directly from it to the painting make your own drawings from the photograph first and work from them. In this way you are carrying your own individuality into the painting rather than merely duplicating the photograph. If you need to refer to the photograph to check values or other details, it is there to help you. But by making a free interpretation, based on the images in the photograph, you will get a better picture than you would by slavishly copying everything the photograph shows.

The way you draw characterizes your work. It is one of its chief means of identification, and has positive value for you and for no one else. For this reason, if for no other, it is foolish to allow another artist's style of drawing to influence you too much. Drawing continually from photographs can be equally bad. If you draw from life the chances are that your work will contain much more individuality than it ever will if you use ready-made drawings or paintings from which proportions can be traced and copied exactly.

A drawing or painting is often more interesting when parts are left unfinished; when certain details are merely suggested by a few pencil or brush strokes. The detail and finish in the other areas will stand out in fine contrast.

A fallacy to which many artists subscribe is that a thing must be depicted so because it is so. If this were necessary, it would deprive us all from using any imagination. Truth can be dramatized, made simpler, glorified, and interpreted according to individual appreciation. The good writer does this all the time. He sticks to essential

Van Gogh . . . sacrificed much to the thing that seemed to enthrall him most—vibrating color

Road with Cypresses by Vincent Van Gogh, MUSEUM OF MODERN ART, NEW YORK CITY.

Marne at Nagent by Raoul Dufy, BIGNOU GALLERY, NEW YORK CITY.   Dufy, in this century, has furthered the impressionist tradition

truth, but expresses it in his own terms. To be outstanding the painter must strive to do the same thing. He will never stir up much commotion if he paints the obvious in the obvious manner. People are not interested in reproductions of what they can see for themselves with their own eyes. Or if they are, then the chances are they would rather look at photographs, which are likely to be more accurate.

We should think about proportion—and drawing as a whole—in the broadest possible terms, making it expressive rather than completely authentic.

The charm of certain cartoons, especially some of the television commercials, lies in expressiveness rather than in realism. The cartoonist would be hopelessly lost if such liberties were denied him. When the cartoonist uses too much realism, the flavor and essence of his art is usually lost, and the result is commonplace and boring.

We must therefore consider drawing and proportion as a means of expression rather than as a blueprint of nature. How we see things and how interestingly we can draw will mean much more to the viewer than how accurately we can draw. Seeing accuracy in all the objects about him, the viewer is much more likely to be interested in the unseen things, the qualities that he has never before attributed to the commonplace.

Only the artist himself can be the judge of how much to distort, how far from the exact to go to stress the theme or spirit of the painting; only he can gauge the dividing line between expressiveness and crudity.

Every artist must develop the ability to draw accurately and well; then he may temper his knowledge to what seems best and most pleasing to him. Distortion that appears in an artist's work because he is unable to draw better has a way of showing up, and it is seldom expressive or inspiring. To be deliberate in distortion takes a great draftsman.

El Greco lengthened his figures purposely to stress his unconventional designs. Michelangelo created heroic figures, enormous of chest, muscle, and body, as forcible symbols of man. Degas stressed the undernourished frailty of some of his little dancers. Daumier went all out to portray character. And the examples of purposeful distortion in modern art are endless.

In most draftsmanship we sense a search for the ideal. Even these artists who make a practice of employing distortion tend to correct what they see in the direction of idealization. We wonder if the models who posed for Sargent always had the beautiful bodies we see in his portraits. Perhaps his idealization accounted for his extreme popularity. His work brought much criticism from the ultra-realists for this reason. My feeling is that Sargent idealized through his innate love of perfection, to make his portraits glorified interpretations of women in general. Some of the portraits done by his contemporaries with great fidelity to life seem rather ordinary by comparison. Most of Sargent's sitters probably are no longer alive, but the glorified interpretation still carries its original charm. Was it not better for time to preserve the beauty of his era than its literal fact?

The danger in too much idealization, of course, is "prettiness," against which much of the revolt of modern art is directed. Idealization often provokes the accusation of insincerity. But does not the crux of the matter lie in whether the actual character of the subject has enough interest in itself? If an accurate portrayal would be insignificant, then there seems to be no harm in the artist's effort to make a more interesting painting. Redesigning, simplification, characterization, even idealization seem warranted. In Sargent's defense let us say that he was perhaps far more interested in the inherent beauty of his canvas than in the beauty of his sitter. If this is a crime, the alternative is to preserve the ordinary.

We must decide in our own minds whether art should be a thing of beauty. If we think so, we must seek to understand what elements contribute to beauty. We must decide whether the thing we are attempting is to be creative or merely to

The Virgin with Saint Ines and Saint Tecla (detail) by El Greco, NATIONAL GALLERY OF ART, WASHINGTON, D. C.   El Greco lengthened his figures purposely to stress his unconventional designs

95

Daumier went all out to portray character

The Lawyers by Honoré Daumier, DURAND-RUEL, INC., NEW YORK CITY.

The Wyndham Sisters by John Singer Sargent, THE METROPOLITAN MUSEUM OF ART, NEW YORK CITY. We wonder if the models who posed for Sargent always had the beautiful bodies we see in his portraits. Perhaps his idealization accounted for his extreme popularity

make a statement of fact, whether we can blend creativeness with fact. Shall we draw as we see or as we feel? What is there about the subject that we can stress? What can we subordinate and simplify elsewhere to make that particular quality stand out? How can we design our subject? What shall we omit and what shall we keep? Shall we make it a composition of close values and quiet beauty or shall we dramatize it with brilliant color and contrast?

What can we think of in the way of technique or texture to make it unusual? Have we chosen a subject that has any interest in itself outside of the execution? Have we experimented with sketches for different interpretations? Have we experimented with the drawing and proportions or with the form to make it more vital? Have we considered the subject as a decoration? Are we making just one more example of something we have done before? Is there enough interest and inspiration in the subject to make us anxious to work on it? Most of all, will the picture stand on its own feet, self-sustaining as to its motif and completeness, or must it forever be explained?

These are the questions that the objective painter may ask himself, and the answers inevitably lead to more creativeness. Let us remember that a landscape need not be an authentic statement of locale. Leave that to the camera. A portrait may well be an expression of a personality rather than a highly accurate likeness. A still life may be an opportunity to express light, form, and color in design, rather than a replica of actual objects. In the same way any subject may be the vehicle for the interpretation of light, atmosphere, form, or color, or simply the means to some sort of striking and unusual design. The creativeness expressed always means more to art than the material used to express it.

Proportion is closely related to rhythm. It is related to design, to character, and to unity. Therefore let us try to establish these relationships wherever our ingenuity can do so. When we consider proportion we should approach it from all angles before we accept it as so just because it is so.

We may say that realism cannot be painted without truth, but then why not enlarge our understanding of truth? The truth is there to help us to greater truth, not to hinder us by the fear of deviating from it. From my point of view, beauty should be the yardstick by which the artist measures truth. Pictures do not have as a reason for their existence the verification of truth; they should be painted to extend beauty in life and to life. Naturally not all truth is beautiful; sordidness and ugliness exist. We may choose to paint them in order to call attention to them, but that is quite a different matter. Many artists have painted ugliness merely as a protest against some particular society that perpetrated it, just as Dickens wrote books to call attention to certain social injustices of his time. This may result in great art, but such works are destined for the museum rather than as decorations for the living-room wall.

It is my contention that the artist seeking beauty will find it and develop it. We all possess it in some degree, and it enlarges and develops by contact. I cannot believe anyone would try to become an artist unless he had some beauty in his soul that he wanted to express. And whether this expression takes the form of realistic or abstract representation is a matter of personal taste.

In the actual laying of paint, which means setting down the masses, realistic and abstract art start out in much the same way. The masses are painted flatly, and while doing this the artist makes a sort of abstraction of the subject to begin with. In some examples of abstract art the artist goes very little further; he makes this suggestion of form. Then he adds a few lines, accents, and highlights. Often he merely lays a sketchy outline drawing over the tones of the masses, without concern that the tone stop at the outline unless he specifically wants it to. There is no reason why the objective painter may not use the same method, or at least borrow the idea. The degree

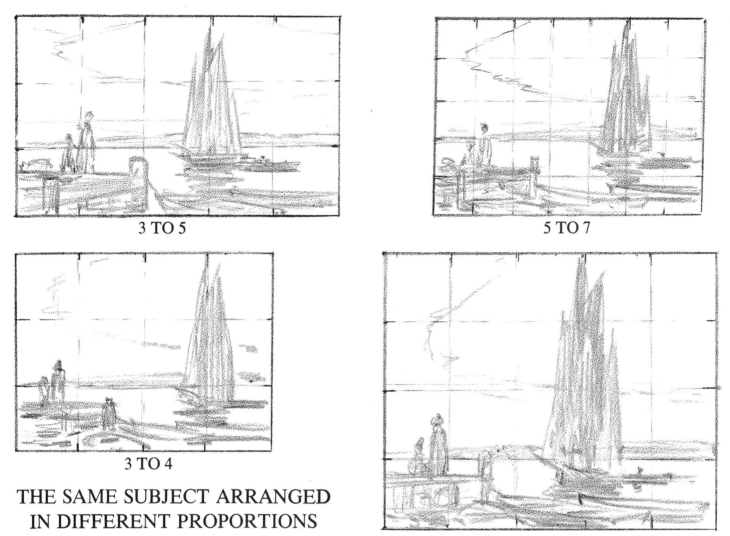

3 TO 5

5 TO 7

3 TO 4

THE SAME SUBJECT ARRANGED
IN DIFFERENT PROPORTIONS

4 TO 5

The drawings above show how the same pictorial materials may be arranged to fit proportionately into pictures of different shapes. Divide the area into squares. Now align the pictorial matter with these divisions. Your eye will tell you when to use the lines or the spaces. Do not use the proportion of two to four, since this results in equal spacing, which generally is not good in any but very formal composition. Four to four and five to seven usually seem to work out best.

to which details are added and contours are more clearly defined is the degree to which an artist is judged as an abstract or realistic painter.

Abstract art is young. It has hardly had time to develop rules, methods, and formula, and the principles used in teaching it probably relate chiefly to dividing space, securing balance, and employing harmonious colors. These basic principles are common to all forms of painting and design.

VII. COLOR

Perhaps the greatest progress art has made through the ages has been in the better understanding and use of color. Color is one element of beauty that stands on its own. When it is combined with design the result can stand alone as art, without adding anything else. But color added to all the other elements of beauty lifts beauty to its highest peak.

Pictorially, value, more than anything else, controls color.

Color cannot be good or correct pictorially unless it has close and correct association with value. Every pictorial color must take its proper place in the value scale, which ranges from the lightest light to darkest dark in any picture. It must belong to the "key" of the subject in order to fit within the chosen range of values. Key and range are discussed in Chapter Eleven, but before we get to that point, there is much to be explained about color.

The colors of the paints we get from the art store bear little or no relationship one to another. We can buy in tubes and jars a great assortment of colors that are quite beautiful when laid out on the palette. These give us a very wide range for choice and mixture, but unfortunately unity, relationship, and harmony of color in a picture are not achieved that way.

When the artist is standing in the art store selecting among these tubes with their intriguing names, he has no way of knowing just what the tones and color of his next subject will be. Of a large collection of various colors only a few may ever be used.

The point is that we do not *buy* shades and tints and variations of color; we produce them on our palette from basic primaries. We actually deal with red, yellow, and blue, and possibly a few earth colors and black to tone them, or raise or lower them in value and intensity.

The only thing we need to know at the color counter is to avoid buying colors that will not mix chemically. Chromes and lead colors are dangerous when not properly mixed, since chemical reactions take place in the mixture. Lead whites discolor in time, especially when mixed with other color. They can also produce lead poisoning in people allergic to lead. These problems are avoided by simply buying Zinc White or Titanium White and mixing it only with cadmiums and colors listed as permanent. Linseed oil has a tendency to yellow. Either turpentine or poppy oil, with a little retouch or dammar varnish for faster drying, is an excellent medium.

Most pictures can be painted with a tube of red, one of yellow, one of blue, one toning agent that is warm, such as burnt sienna or burnt umber, and another that is cool, such as black or blue-black. Which red, yellow, and blue you select depends more on the subject than on the name of the color.

A full palette contains a warm and cool of each primary, plus toners. A warm yellow is a yellow that leans toward orange or red, such as cadmium yellow or cadmium medium yellow. A cool yellow leans toward green, as does cadmium pale or cadmium lemon. A warm blue leans toward green, as cerulean blue, and the cobalts. A cool blue leans toward violet, as ultramarine blue or permanent blue. In the reds, cadmium red or Indian red is warm; Alizarin Crimson or Crimson Lake, cool.

This means two reds, two yellows, and two blues. Yellow ochre is really a low-toned yellow and may be used in flesh tones and warm grays. Burnt sienna may be added to the yellows, reds, and oranges to lower them in value and retain their brilliancy. Black has a tendency to neutralize the warm colors, but will lower the cool colors, the blues, greens, and violets, without destroying the identity of the color.

The greatest mistake in color, and one that causes lack of unity and harmony, usually results from having too many colors on the palette. When the secondary colors, the greens, oranges, and violets, are mixed from the primaries on the palette, a relationship is established. It is better not to buy an array of greens or violets. Cadmium orange, however, is related to cadmium red or cadmium yellow, since they are ground from the same pigment.

With a palette set up with a warm and cool of each primary, plus white and the toning colors, practically any color or tint of color may be mixed. Any shade of every color in the light and dark scales can be obtained. And color may be neutralized to produce any gray in any value.

A picture painted with one of each of the three primaries will usually be more harmonious than one painted with two of each. If all six colors are used, the picture will be more intense and brilliant. But, strangely enough, the more we know about color, the fewer colors we use. Great painters usually use quite simple palettes. When we realize that all the color evident in some of the brilliant color film of today springs from three dyes we begin to understand the possibilities. But the color in film is transparent and is greatly increased in brilliance by the strong light of the projector. Except for transparent watercolor, the artist's color is for the most part opaque. The light we see in a picture is reflected light, whatever the source, and cannot be as brilliant as sunlight or any direct light.

Colors in almost their pure state, when laid side by side and at a little distance, will mix to produce other colors in the eye. The difficulty lies in making the values of these colors nearly identical, so that the effect does not become spotty and the tonal value of the area is maintained. A pink laid next to a blue of the same value will produce a much lovelier lavender color than can be obtained by mixing red, white, and blue on the palette. A red on the warm side can be laid beside a red on the cool side with much more beautiful effect than either would give alone.

All this is known as "broken color." We can reduce or "gray" a color by using it with its complementary color in the same value, and intensify it by using it with a color lying close to it on the color wheel. Thus red is toned down by associating it with its complement green, and intensified by using orange or cooler red in conjunction with it. The same is true of the other colors: yellow green and yellow orange intensify yellow; blue green and blue violet intensify blue. To neutralize yellow we use violet; to neutralize blue, orange. But we must match the values or the effect will be spotty and broken.

For this discovery in the use of color, Van Gogh perhaps deserves a little more credit than some other painters, but the whole group of impressionist and postimpressionist painters unquestionably made great contributions.

A great deal of experiment is needed to perfect this method of using color. The broken color may be tried out on separate boards before being laid into the actual painting.

The best procedure is to mix colors on the palette to get a tone as close as possible in color and value to what we see, then set down a mass in this tone. Into this neutralized color we then lay in separately, as broken color, the colors we mixed to get this tone. This, which I call the second painting, or the "go over" of the original masses, can be done either while the area is still wet or after it has dried.

The impressionists often painted their broken color directly onto the bare canvas. If we follow this procedure we are likely to miss the value that an undertone or mass will give us. Since values are very difficult to lighten or darken after they have been painted with broken color, I believe the other approach is better as a general practice. If broken color is to retain its brilliance and vitality it has to be left very much alone. If the values are not right, it is better to scrape it out and start over, instead of trying to change the value. The latter procedure is almost sure to get messy.

In painting broken color into a tone, we have the advantage of the grayer color underneath to enhance and enrich the more brilliant color on top. The undertone helps to hold the broken color together in unity.

If a canvas is to be varnished, the color can be enriched after it dries by glazing pure color diluted with varnish over the dry color. This can only be done if the whole canvas is to be varnished; otherwise part of the picture may have a mat finish, while the glazed color will dry shiny. A picture should be either all mat or all varnished.

A third way of producing broken color, and one of the best, is to build up a surface on the canvas, and drag color over it, so that it picks up nodules of color from the brush, which are laid over other colors. The built-up surface can be made by underpainting with a fast-drying white. There are several of these underpainting mediums on the market. Gesso may be used if a good bond is established between the gesso and the painting surface. After such a built-up surface is dry it may be stained with an undertone, then the broken color dragged over it, allowing the high points of the underpainting to catch the paint from the brush. Such overpainting is done with thickly mixed paint. Thin paint would only fill in the rough surface flatly.

It is also possible to combine these methods. Where you have a smooth undersurface, perhaps a sky, you can paint in your broken color. Where the surface is rough, as in the foreground, you may drag on the color. Variety of technique in a single painting is not only permissible, but often necessary to achieve the manifold textural effects that nature presents. However they must be combined with care to give an all-over effect of unity.

In planning a picture, or when building up an undersurface, it should be planned so that the shadow areas can be painted thinly. You do not want a lot of points or bumps of pigment sticking out in the shadow area and catching highlights. For the most part highly textured painting should be used for landscapes, marines, and still lifes. If you are painting flesh, too much texture (and I speak of it here only in relation to color) can be out of place.

Color harmony is vital to the success of any painting, and to understand it we must analyze the possible combinations of color. Any two of the three primaries—red, yellow, and blue—can be combined to produce one of the secondaries. Red and yellow produce orange; red and blue, purple or violet; yellow and blue, green. Orange, purple or violet, and green are the complements, respectively, of blue, yellow, and red. The tertiaries are made up of two parts of one primary to one part of another. Two parts of red and one of blue give red purple; two parts of blue and one of red, blue violet. Red orange is two parts red and one part yellow; yellow orange, two yellow and one red. Blue green is two parts blue and one yellow; yellow green two parts yellow and one blue. These are all pure mixtures.

Now if we mix a primary with its complement we produce brown, or neutralized color. This will be the same in each case if the mixture is equal. Yellow plus its complement purple is in reality yellow plus red plus blue, since purple consists of equal parts of red and blue. Red plus its complement green is red plus yellow plus blue. Blue plus its complement orange is blue plus red plus yellow. Obviously they all add up to the same thing and to the same color of brown. But we can tone a color with its complement to reduce it in intensity, and by degrees arrive at a tremendous range of colors, all of which are related, since each will contain some fraction of the original three primaries. We can tone a color either by this method or by adding actual brown or cold black.

This is what happens in a color transparency. The various degrees of mixture of the three colors produce every other color, even to browns, apparent blacks, and grayed tints. The same thing is true of halftone printing in color. Reproductions of paintings are printed with four separate plates using red, yellow, blue, and black ink. The black plate is used as a key plate to give these colors richness and depth.

Since the colors of the spectrum are easy to recognize, painting would not be difficult if everything were pure in color. But only man-made things are; in nature, the vast majority of colors are grays which lean toward the primaries. We separate them by considering them as warm and cool. We have, for example, gray greens, or greens that are somewhat neutralized. We have greens that tend toward the yellow and those that lean toward the blue. In the same way, all the other secondary and tertiary colors may be neutralized or may tend toward the primaries from which they are produced. When we think of colors in this way they are much easier to "see" and the eye can be trained to recognize the ingredients.

Whether we mix the colors on the palette or within the painting is a matter of choice. When one area looks warmer than another area that is supposed to match it in color, we can add some red yellow or orange to the second area. The addition may be very slight. Or when the color in one area appears cooler by comparison with another, we can add a little blue, blue green, or violet to the other. Since black mixes with white to form a rather bluish gray, we may even add a touch of

black to a color to cool it, or at least a gray mixed from black and white.

The finest painters have handed down the rule that all three primaries should never appear in their full strength within the same picture. Since they are not basically related they have a tendency to fight one another. They can easily be brought into harmony by mixing a little of one into the other two, or at least into one of the others. This leaves one as dominant, and makes the other two related even if they are only slightly reduced in brilliancy. This does not mean that one primary color must dominate the picture or design. We are simply tempering the colors to bring them into harmony. We can extend the influence if we wish by adding a little of one secondary or tertiary color to all the others.

A late-afternoon landscape could thus have a touch of yellow or orange added to all the other colors. In this way we achieve the relationship and unity brought about by the warmth of the late-afternoon sun, and gain the "feel" of the scene.

This rule applies equally to all subjects, since there should be unity in all painting. Painting into wet tone does much the same thing in uniting color, provided a little of the tone mixes with the color. Tempering the white with a little color is another way of achieving unity.

Before choosing a color to use in a painting we should first analyze its hue, or the color toward which it seems to lean, and its value in the black-and-white scale. Ordinarily the purer colors are kept for spots to be set into the more neutral colors. This is exactly the procedure used by the modern interior decorator. He may choose to give one wall more color than the others, to avoid the feeling of being closed in on four sides by the same value and color. But brilliant color on all four walls is hard to live with unless some relief in softer and grayer color accompanies it. We might put a red carpet in a gray room, or a gray one in a red room, but we would be very uncomfortable if everything were red.

The Café at Night by Vincent Van Gogh, Walter A. Curtin, photographer,
KRÖLLER-MULLER MUSEUM, OTTERLO, HOLLAND

Early Sunday Morning by Edward Hopper, COLLECTION OF THE WHITNEY MUSEUM OF AMERICAN ART

Light in Autumn by William Thon, DR. AND MRS. MORTIMER N. HYAMS, NEW YORK CITY

The Helicopter by Dong Kingman

Egg Beater III by Stuart Davis, William H. Lane Foundation, courtesy of the DOWNTOWN GALLERY

This leads us to color "balance." There was a period of painting when all shadow was treated as brown, instead of as a deeper tone of the local color, or with the local color still in evidence in the shadow. This style of painting was known as the "brown school." When all the color in a painting belongs to only one side of the color wheel, muddiness, monotony, and lack of color appeal almost always result. Happily no one paints that way today.

Color balance means a happy relationship of the warm versus the cool. The difference need not extend to pure primaries, but some contrast is needed for balance. Outdoors the sky usually takes care of this, along with the coolness brought about by the atmosphere. The blue of the sky finds its way into the shadows by reflection, and the atmosphere of the distance provides cool contrast to the warm colors of the foreground.

Indoors, shadows are more neutral. By contrast with the cool north light of the studio, they may well appear somewhat warmer. However, in parts of the house where sunlight enters and glimpses of the outdoors may be seen, the balance of warm and cool is more evident.

So we may consider the warmth and coolness of the masses as opposed to each other but also reach for the play of warm and cool color together and within the masses.

It is much easier to determine the true color and value of an area when it is seen in company with other tones. A single color on a card may look very different from the same color laid into the picture. We should always start a picture by stating three or more adjacent values and colors, rather than by laying in one area and filling it in, then looking at another area and doing the same thing. By finding a spot in the picture where two or three values come together, we can then spread these values one against another and establish the relationship of all the big masses. A young painter will often fill in and almost finish one area before starting another. This is the method used in much commercial art and one of the main reasons such work seldom achieves good relationship, harmony, and unity. We cannot know whether values are right and in proper brilliancy and contrast until we see them together.

Perhaps the biggest mistake made in the rendering of color is in color within shadow. Many artists simply lighten the pure color with white for the lights, and use the pure color for the shadows. This is just the opposite of what occurs in life. The purest color belongs to the light, and the shadows are more neutral, having less color than the lighted areas. For example, to paint a blue dress pale blue in the light, and a purer and more intense or darker tone of the same color in the shadow is entirely false. The dress must either be pale blue all over, or strong blue all over. To paint the shadows in a pale blue dress we add the complement or a toner to the color. This keeps the brighter, purer color in the light where it belongs. If we use a stronger, purer blue in the lighted areas, we probably need to add some black to the shadows.

In commercial art we often see pink lights on red dresses. But red is reddest in the light. We see orange shadows on a yellow sweater, when they should be yellow reduced with its complement, violet. We see flesh painted pink in the light and red in the shadow. All this is false and cheapens the finished work. It is based on a mistaken idea that lightening the light areas keeps the color clean, whereas what really keeps color clean is the right relationship of color and value.

When color is grayed and softened by the use of toners or complements it takes on quality. A color appears dull only if its neighbors are too brilliant or out of value. When a young artist is advised to tone his colors, he often misinterprets the advice and thinks that he has been asked to use dull colors. Strangely, the toned color seems to end up with more over-all brilliance than the pure colors, which actually work against one another. Pictures are brightened much more by contrasting good values than by piling in more and more pure color. But this fact is hard to believe until it has been proved by personal experiment.

Once in a while in commercial art we see an underlying drawing in which all the shadows are black or nearly black and the color has been put into the lighted areas later. This technique sometimes results in powerful and attractive work. While all shadows are not black, (nor do we always want to paint them that way), the effect is far better than that of pictures in which the shadows are all painted in pure color. The reason is simply that it is more consistent and truthful to have the color brightest in the light. The black shadows are more neutralized. Again, in a very powerful light the shadows may appear almost black by contrast, and because our value range in pigment is limited.

In laying in the shadow masses of any picture it is a good idea to paint them in richly and darkly. They can all be lightened where necessary, to bring the relationships of light and shadow to what they should be. While a white shirt or any white object could never actually have a black shadow, the contrast in a brilliant light without much reflected light in the shadow can be quite surprising.

There are many qualities of color which the old masters knew how to reproduce, and which most modern painters appear to have overlooked or forgotten. There is a particular quality of "radiance," for instance, which we find in the greatest works of the past. Rembrandt still realized this quality and went far in developing it, but it seems to have gradually disappeared from the work of later painters. This quality assuredly exists in nature but is more felt than seen, except by the most skillful and practiced eye. To describe it in words is extremely difficult. It is light visually cast into space by light itself. This does not mean the effect of reflected light on other objects, but light surrounding and emanating from its source.

We know that the air is filled with minute particles which have the property of picking up light

and reflecting it between the source and the surface upon which it falls. In very bright light such as sunlight or the beam of a searchlight or projector we may see the stream of light passing through the atmosphere. But now think of the surface that is being lighted. This becomes a secondary source of light, casting it away from the surface, so that it strikes the particles in the air around it.

Thus a certain amount of halation, of which we are not always aware, surrounds all lighted surfaces. We see a blur of light around a headlight, or even around a candle flame, and we would normally show this in painting. But a lesser degree of this same halation is not so obvious. Such halation traverses its boundaries or the edges of the lighted area. The edge itself may be quite distinct and sharply defined, but the space around the edge becomes lighted also.

A bright moon may appear as sharply outlined against the background of space. But if we look carefully we see that there is a gradation of light over the whole moonlit sky, which grows brighter as it approaches the source. The same thing happens with a strongly lighted head against a dark background. The dark lightens as it approaches the head, or a white area, or even any brightly lighted surface. Such lightening is hardly perceptible until we train our eyes to be conscious of it.

What is more, the *color* of the light source extends itself into surrounding space. This is actually a color influence rather than a repeated color. The color of the light blends into the color of the background. Paintings can be given a wholly new quality of radiance when this phenomenon is studied and reproduced. It is a further method of relating color to its environment and of unifying the surrounding area.

A colored spotlight projects color in a visible stream through the dark of the theater to the stage. The spotlight, of course, has been focused to condense the light rays. The lighted surface, however, sends its almost invisible rays in all directions. Therefore the only way we can render it is as a slight radiation of light into all surrounding form and space.

A very good example is to be found in the way the old masters painted a light emanating from the cradle of the Christ-child, and sometimes from the body of Christ. If you study the work of Rembrandt carefully, you will find this understanding of light even in his etchings. The quality of radiance in his work is one reason for their recognition as great masterpieces.

"Radiance" is a better term than "halation" to describe this phenomenon, for halation may be obvious and appear simply as a blurred edge.

This use of light does not mean that the edge should be blurred into the background. The edge is held, but the background is lighter next to the light than it is elsewhere. We should remember that the sky casts this light and color down into the landscape, wherever strong sunlight does not overpower the effect. The ground plane also throws its light and color upward into otherwise dark shadows of underplanes, and even onto some of the vertical planes. In such a manner an old barn can be united to the sunlit ground it stands on, or a head can be united to a dark hairdress, or a white collar or bosom can be united to a dark costume. Study Velásquez for this quality, and also Carolus Duran, Sargent, and Vermeer.

Another consideration in connection with color is concentration. When possible, brilliant color should be concentrated in the area of greatest interest and not scattered. A vase of flowers will command interest and attention in a room because of its bright color; similarly in a painting, the brightest color should be associated with the dominant figure or object. This does not mean the entire object should necessarily be bright in color, but some portion of it should be in high focus. Surrounding colors may be grayed or neutralized to keep the emphasis where it is wanted. In still lifes, the bright color is usually concentrated in fruit or flowers. In landscapes, bright color may be concentrated in the sails of boats, flowers, sunset clouds, costumes, or other such features.

Color can also be intensified along the edges of certain objects to make them stand out more strongly in a painting. Holes between branches through which sky appears may be surrounded by more vivid blue than that of the sky showing through, painted into the darks surrounding the opening. An area of color can be brightened considerably by adding its next neighbor in the color wheel to the edge of the area. For example, a patch of yellow can be intensified by putting yellow orange or yellow green at the edge where it meets the next pattern. A sky can be made a bit stronger in color where it meets a white cloud. A red garment might have a little red purple introduced at the edges. Intensifying the color of edges will brighten an otherwise dull subject.

Color lends itself to experiment more than does any other element of beauty. If anyone were to ask me to list the greatest gifts of nature to man, I would place color at the top, or very near to it. Art without color would lose much of its purpose. By devoting ourselves to color, we can enrich our art and our lives with it beyond measure.

VIII. RHYTHM

Rhythm in nature is another element of beauty, one that is perhaps more felt than seen. There is rhythm of line, of form, of color, and even of values. In music rhythm is the tempo, the beat—the swing, as we call it now. In art it is the flow of repetitious line, the sweep of movement within the design and arrangement. A line may continue its movement, disappear, and be picked up again elsewhere, to carry out the main lines of a design. This is true in almost any pose of the human figure. But there is rhythm in other forms, as well. It is typical of all forms of growth. There is rhythm in the arrangement of bark on a tree, as well as in the branches. There is rhythm of line and form in all animal life.

In order to study rhythm in growing things we look at the edges of mass and form to find the main direction of line. Then we follow that direction, skipping across the form if necessary, to find whether the line can be picked up again, and either continued in the same direction or swung gracefully in another direction.

The sparks flying off a pinwheel make a good illustration of rhythm. The circular motion is gently carried out into space. Rhythm is very apparent in the eddies and flow of water. There is rhythm in the strands and flow of a woman's hair. There is rhythm in the shavings curling off the carpenter's plane. But we must do more than look for obvious rhythms. Sometimes we must deliberately create rhythm, by adjusting the line and form we see to include this unifying element.

In drawing rhythmic forms we must be sure to give them stability by establishing contrasting horizontal, vertical, or diagonal lines in the picture. If there were nothing but curve and movement the result would be a veritable cyclone of movement which would be both unrealistic and unpleasant. However in most pictures rhythm is more likely to be missing than excessive. Comfortable rhythm in drawing is a happy combination of curved lines with straight. Sometimes more solidity and structure is added by drawing curves with straight blocky lines. But the relation of the rhythm of one form to that of another should always be in evidence.

Rhythm is achieved by noting how one part fits into another, and thus joining all the parts to create the whole. In the human body the limbs unite beautifully with the torso, merging form with form. We seek to unite the forms in the ground plane of a landscape, and to join the hills and mountains to these. The base of a hill or mountain usually has a sweep where the sharp slant slopes off gradually to meet the lower ground. We find this same sweep of line from the vertical to the horizontal in the roots of a tree as they spread to meet the ground. There is rhythm in rock strata, and there is much of it to be found in cloud forms. Poetic license can be taken by the artist in exaggerating the rhythm of any object where a more graceful or dramatic picture will be the result.

We should always group the material so that the patterns of our subjects unite gracefully and beautifully and so the edges are woven together in repetitive or long flowing lines.

Upside Down Table and Mask by Yasuo Kuniyoshi, DOWNTOWN
GALLERY, NEW YORK CITY. In drawing rhythmic forms we must be
sure to give them stability by establishing contrasting horizontal,
vertical, or diagonal lines in the picture

Expectation by Frederic Taubes, ASSOCIATED AMERICAN ARTISTS, NEW YORK CITY.   Comfortable rhythm in drawing is a happy combination of curved lines with straight

RHYTHM

A linear analysis of paintings by the old masters can be useful. And so can the study of oriental art, where rhythmic line plays such an important part in drawings and paintings. For actual practice, take any photograph and trace rhythmic lines over it to create a more unified and exciting design.

If you are painting a still life, watch for rhythmic lines in the arrangement. A line may be picked up in the folds of a drapery, and allowed to flow gracefully out of the arrangement. In still life the objects may be so placed that the contours of the group are suitably related to one another. Flowers can be arranged so the blossoms and stems repeat or extend the lines of the vase in which they are placed.

I think one of the most beautiful instances of rhythm is the uniting of the loose material of a costume with the more tightly fitted material over the form of a body. This is really uniting the body with the costume. Because of this rhythmic relationship, a garment is much more beautiful on a body than by itself. Even the law of gravity seems to create rhythm in the shapes that a fabric takes, all in relationship to one another.

Rhythm in growth is illustrated by the way the leaves of plants are arranged around the stems or stalks, and by the position of the petals on a flower. Clouds arrange themselves with rhythmic lines according to the direction of the wind. Water does the same. If we cast a stone into still water the rhythmic motion begins. A second stone will cause rhythms that beautifully transverse the first ones. The wake of a boat streams out in beautiful rhythm in direct relation to the direction and even to the speed of the boat.

Rhythm is not confined to line; it exists in color too. One is united to another through the colors of the spectrum. Thus we may move through red orange to orange, to yellow orange, to yellow. Then from yellow we move to blue by going through the intermediate tones in sequence. Therefore if you have two widely separated colors in a subject, you may adroitly incorporate the natural sequence of the colors between them. These need not necessarily touch, but be placed close enough to establish continuity and rhythm between the two unrelated colors. This applies to designs as well as to pictorial subjects. Good use can be made of the transition of color at the edges of a pattern.

The same sort of thing can be done with values. When there are two widely separated values we can contrive to get some of the intervening values into the picture, to alleviate harshness. This occurs in nature with the halftone gradations between light and shadow, and with reflected light. Even within shadow there is usually some variation in tone. Although we try to keep our shadows simple, we seldom paint them black or completely flat in value.

Both in values and in color, rhythm is also produced by repetition. A bright color is usually repeated somewhere else, perhaps reduced a little and not left as an isolated spot. By adding the near relatives of the color somewhere else in the same subject we bring unity and rhythm to our picture. For example, in a portrait the flesh colors of the head and neck are usually repeated effectively on the arms and hands.

Color rhythm is also produced by varying the color but sustaining the value, as in broken color.

Examine a flower closely and you will notice that the color varies within the flower and is often repeated in the stems and foliage. This color pigment has so to speak flowed through the plant to appear in varying degrees through foliage and flower. Thus the leaves become related to the flower in color. You could not transpose the flower of one plant to the stem and leaves of another variety and keep the same harmony.

The rhythm of color is something like that of sound. We know that sound travels in rhythmic vibrations or waves. Color does the same thing. Every color has its individual rhythm of waves or vibrations which register in the eye as that color. There is a definite connection or relationship between sound, color, and light. All operate on vibrations but at tremendously different speeds.

Today there are methods of drawing, some of them quite remarkable, in which the artist, without looking at the paper, tries to move his hand in the rhythms he sees in the subject before him, allowing the pencil to set these rhythms down continuously on the drawing surface. I find that I have to look at the paper in order to hold one part in proportion to another, because I have never trained my hand to "feel" these rhythms as my eye sees them. But it can be done. Those who are interested in learning to draw in this manner should read *The Natural Way to Draw* by Kimon Nicolaides.[1] It is a wonderful book.

At first it is natural to think of scrolls or ornament of one kind or another in connection with rhythm. But rhythm is more beautiful when it is not obvious. It is more concerned with the underlying structure of a composition than with the surface detail. This is what is meant by rhythm's being more felt than seen.

It is good practice to lay a few curves that seem related to each other on your drawing surface, then see if you can subtly build in your subject over these curves. Parts, of course, may vary from these lines, but the curve or line is picked up somewhere beyond these protruding or overlapping parts. See also how far you can go in including the natural sequences of color in the spectrum or color wheel. A sky may be a purplish blue at the very top, where the deepest tone is to be seen, and the color may then move downward through blue into bluish green, and finally to a greenish tone near the horizon. The distance starts at the horizon with blues and blue purples, then nearer to us come the blue greens and warmer greens, and finally the yellows, oranges, and reds, associated with the near foreground. You will note that this includes most of the spectrum colors; and this is one of the great secrets of nature's color. The colors you use in your painting need not be the spectrum colors in

[1] Boston: Houghton Mifflin Company, 1941.

their pure state, but softer reduced tones of these brighter colors.

Always associated with these colors is a similar sequence of values which makes color seem to flow through the subject rhythmically instead of jumping about without relationship.

Let us also consider the emotional effects of rhythm. We know how painful it is to listen to a pianist who has little or no sense of rhythm. While rhythm in painting is much more subtle, its absence can be equally unfortunate. Much modern art is constructed only upon straight lines, with many sharp angles and little or nothing to relieve them. Sometimes blocks are piled upon blocks without proper regard for structure. Such artists should take greater note of how the bricklayer staggers his joints for unity and strength. This staggering actually binds the shapes together, rhythmically, as well as making a stronger wall.

However, exact duplication of line or form usually becomes monotonous when repeated over and over. Where it is necessary, such as in the pattern of a soundly constructed wall, we accept it, but if the rhythms in a mountain crest, for instance, were made identical, we would find such a picture very uninteresting. Furthermore it would be inaccurate. Rhythms in nature repeat, but never in identical shape. There are always smaller waves with large ones. There are bushes with trees, and the forms in one tree, though similar, never exactly duplicate those in another. Big stones are strewn with small ones, all of different shapes. When there must be repetition of line and form in a subject, the artist should strive to give it variety by size, grouping, color, value, or in any other manner.

As we produce variety in the shapes and areas of our patterns, this same kind of variety should appear in the pictorial material itself. Rhythm pictorially need not be a representation of actual movement, but a suggestion of movement in line and form. This is in the sense that the letter S suggests movement while the letters T and L are static. Sometimes I think the letter S might have derived from the movement of a snake. At least the snake in movement is one of the most perfect examples of rhythm.

The deeper we look into the subject of rhythm, the more we realize that everything living, and the universe itself, pulsates with it. There is rhythm in breathing, in walking or running. Days and nights, months and years, follow in rhythmic cycles. Rhythm is what gives life to a picture, and when we realize this fully we will never again allow ourselves to paint a static picture.

IX. FORM

The subject of form is a controversial one today, and there is considerable leeway in its interpretation. Among the modern painters there are some who argue that form should not be represented in three dimensions on a flat plane because it is inconsistent with the two-dimensional surface. These artists believe that three-dimensional form should be reserved for sculpture. The argument is at least interesting and on the surface seems quite logical.

However the assertion that three-dimensional form cannot be represented on a flat plane is based upon a very literal kind of truth. A painting is not necessarily a matter of materialistic truth, requiring that a thing of bulk and dimension must actually be reduced to a plane as an ingot of iron is rolled into sheet metal. A painting is a thing of illusion. A reflection of a face in a mirror literally and actually lies on a flat plane, but it gives the illusion of a third dimension. A photograph also lies on a flat plane and creates the same illusion. So does good painting. The men who argue that form should not be represented on a flat plane have not searched deeply enough for truth, they are accepting only material fact. Beyond all this is the even bigger truth that man's creativity must not and cannot be limited to factual truth, for every now and then creativity will transcend fact.

We know that basically form is substance, and that it can be created in actuality or by illusion. Form need not lose its visual properties in painting, since it is only its appearance that is made known to us by the eye. It must be touched in order for us to sense its bulk and dimensions. Therefore form as seen is really an illusion of our own eyes and brain just as it is in the mirror. We cannot be wrong by painting it as it looks, for we are concerned here with something else. We may represent it in one of two ways, either by a flat diagram as in a blueprint, or as it appears to the eye. Any pictorial representation of form must be one, the other, or some degree of variation between the two. It can be redesigned in either way; it can be visually true or it can be purposely distorted. The artist may choose to represent the decorative quality of flattened form or else to create the complete illusion of the solid aspect of form within space.

Form as interpreted in abstract painting is so much a matter of personal approach that no instruction can prove very helpful. But the elements of beauty, which are themselves abstractions, give us objectives to strive toward in this kind of painting as in any other. There is no reason why the color cannot be harmonious, the design and pattern beautiful, or why symbolism cannot be introduced, the emotional effects of line injected, and the decorative quality stressed to achieve unity throughout our abstract compositions.

In dealing with form in realistic painting, we must of course rely on the correct interpretation of light and color. Front or back lighting produces a simplified statement of form. Three-quarter lightings produce more variations of light and shadow and therefore increase the solid or

114

NOT THIS   ORGANIZE THE SHAPES   LOOK FOR BLOCK FORMS

NOR THIS   GET FULL RANGE OF VALUES   TRY TO SEE THE MASSES

TRAINING THE EYE TO SEE THE FORM WITHIN CONTOURS

The difference between good and bad drawing or painting is not always in contour and detail, as many think, but in the way the subject has been seen. If one looks only at contours and detail, the drawing may come out like the tree and the head shown at left of the above illustration. We must learn to look for the masses and values that define the form—light, halftone, and shadow as they occur on form. Sometimes we must go even further and attempt to group, design, or organize what we see into even simpler planes and masses. Simple outline is better than outline accompanied by unrelated and misunderstood values.

three-dimensional effect. With diffused light the gradations of light to shadow are much more subtle and have less contrast. The important thing is to choose the kind of lighting that will make our subjects most beautiful and suit the composition we have chosen to make.

When the light can be controlled, it is a good idea to experiment with the material at hand under different degrees and angles of light before you start to paint.

If you are making a simple design or pattern, direct front lighting or diffused light will serve your purpose best. If you want a picture that is bright and sparkling with highlights, top or back lighting would be a logical choice.

An artist's painting made against the light will usually have more sparkle than one he executes with the light behind him. This is because the top planes will be brilliantly lighted, setting objects out in relief. Just as sunlight or moonlight creates a path of sparkling light on water, it will do so on forms such as rocks, foliage, or figures.

Direct side or right-angle lightings divide the subject into equal light and shadow, whereas most artists feel that one should dominate the other.

From the point of view of form, three-quarter lighting, from either front or back, is perhaps the most interesting. This kind of lighting displays forms in all their variety and shape. The accompanying technical problems presented under these conditions are proportionately greater for the artist, but he can only gain by making the experiment.

It is true that suggested form is more interesting than form finished to the last detail, but such interpretation requires a more imaginative approach and a looser technique. Some artists achieve this technique easily; others slave for it for years, and may never attain it. The reason suggestion is often more effective than a literal statement is that it calls equally upon the imagination of the viewer.

To create an impression of form we must stop before the interpretation is complete. We may do this by not filling in the mass entirely. We may leave little breaks in the halftone, or not brush over it solidly and completely, or we may make a sharper and more chiseled break into the shadow. Brush strokes can be left showing where the actual form is perfectly smooth and edges can be lost where such omissions effectively emphasize some other and more important feature.

Impressionistic painting makes use of many happy, accidental effects, and the wise artist will train himself to leave well alone. If he does not approach his work in this way, but paints meticulously inch by inch, he is unlikely to produce such accidentals which give spontaneity and life to a subject. There is not much any artist can do to retrieve the feeling of spontaneity in a painting once this quality has been lost.

It is best to think of each subject and each painting as an entirely separate affair. One subject may call for one kind of treatment and another one for an altogether different technique. If the subject at hand calls for exactness, do not refrain from using detail simply because you rather liked the lack of it in something else you did once. Norman Rockwell likes detail. He has built a reputation from it. It is foolish to criticize his work for that reason. If Rockwell wants to develop other qualities in his work, only he can do it. But if he enjoys detail, he is being himself by painting it, which in the long run is the best thing any artist can be. Raoul Dufy was not interested in detail. He liked to paint loosely, using light and sunny colors to depict outdoor scenes on the shore, on the racetrack, and elsewhere in France. He too was being himself. If you are not yourself, you cannot be anyone else, and can easily end up by being nobody in particular.

One can learn a great deal about form by painting a wide range of different forms, from human faces to glass bowls and from barns to city skyscrapers. In each case, it is of first importance to try to make what we paint look convincing. A piece of pottery has an identifying character in

Young Henry Ford by Norman Rockwell, FORD MOTOR COMPANY.   Norman Rockwell likes detail. . . . He is being himself by painting it, which in the long run is the best thing any artist can be

This sort of idealization was carried out in **Greek and Roman** sculpture. We call it "classic," which to me means **the greatest possible beauty** that can be achieved with a certain kind of form

Venus of Cirene (Greco-Roman), ROME.

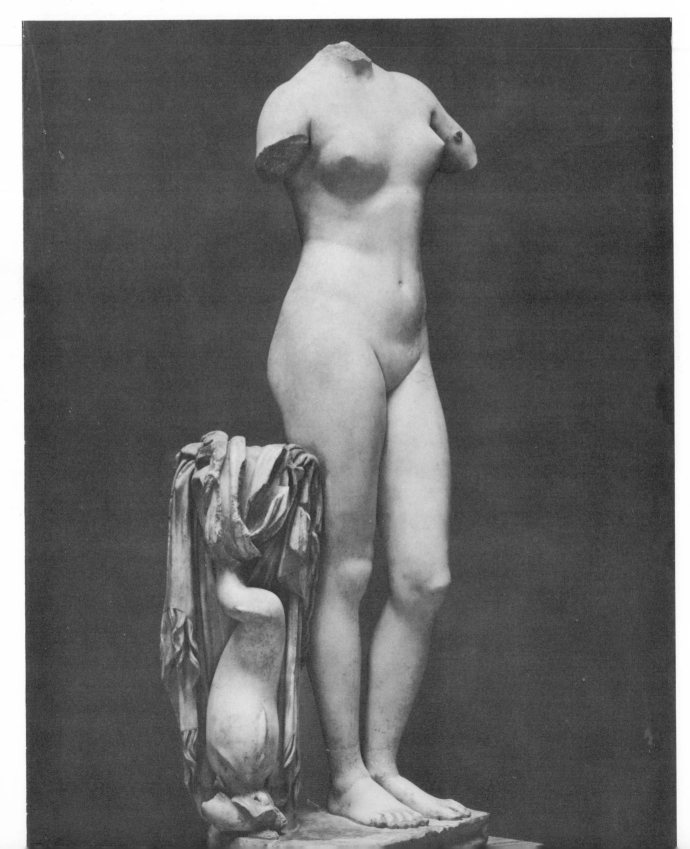

Music by Eugene Berman, JULIEN LEVY. It is true that suggested form is more interesting than form finished to the last detail, but such interpretation requires a more imaginative approach and a looser technique. Some artists achieve this technique easily; others slave for it for years, and **may never attain it**

119

its surface, its values, its color, and the way it looks in different kinds of light. Flesh, to look like flesh, must be painted very differently from the way we would paint a piece of wood which in turn has its own characteristics. A cotton dress cannot be painted in the same way we would paint one that was made of silk or satin. Each object has a characteristic color and texture as well as an identifiable shape.

To the layman form is merely shape and material. To the artist form is also light, halftone, and shadow, in subtle and refined relationships. The shape is there, but it underlies everything else. An object in one light and in a certain location cannot be transposed to another setting without a corresponding change in light and space relationships.

In order to paint form with solidity we must seek out the planes and set them into the proper sequence of values. The plane at right angles to the source of light is the lightest and brightest. As the planes turn from this source they change in value until they reach the shadow. Thus the solidity of the form becomes evident. The shape of the shadow identifies the shape of the form, and the shadow cast on other surfaces relates the form to its environment. In a diffused light, there is still the change of plane, but being much more subtle and without cast shadow, it must be related to its environment by the relationship of its values to the values around it.

To return for a moment to the question of idealized form, we must remember that by idealizing it we may lose its inherent character, and that character actually may be more beautiful than any "improved" or "slicked over" effect we might add. Even if we paint only an impression, it should be an honest one. Beauty may be found in idealization, but we must not forget that it also is found in truth.

But the idealization of form need not mean "prettying" a subject up; it may merely involve the process of simplification. It can mean the flattening of the round into planes; it can mean stressing design or the elimination of nonessential and distracting details so that the basic structure of a beautiful object is properly revealed.

This sort of idealization was carried out in Greek and Roman sculpture. We call it "classic," which to me means the greatest possible beauty that can be achieved with a certain kind of form; in ordinary language, it is "tops" in its class.

X. TEXTURE

Texture, since it is a matter of surface, is more closely related to character than it is to form. Light delineates texture as it does form, and its reflection on a surface creates color. Without light there is no color.

While color can always be applied in smooth flat tones on the canvas, the rendering of different textures requires a variety of brushes and techniques. However, texture can often be suggested rather than copied in a detailed manner. If we follow the effect of a texture in light and color we can come very close to rendering it, even on a smooth canvas. Thus texture in painting does not necessarily mean that the surface has to be built up with layers of paint. At times, however, under-surface painting can greatly enhance certain textural effects. Heavy underpainting usually provides so-called "accidentals" which are textural rather than flat in treatment, and which otherwise might have to be done very painstakingly with small brushes to no better or less good effect. The texture of the canvas itself may be transposed to the painting and fairly well controlled by the way the paint is applied. In the parts of a rough canvas where we want a smooth texture, as in the sky, we simply fill in the grain of the canvas surface with thinner paint. Thicker, drier pigment is used for heavy textural effects such as might be needed for bushes or woodland foliage, and the paint must be allowed to dry between layers of color.

Some of the most interesting textures in painting can be achieved by using a palette knife, dragging the knife over the surface and letting the paint cling to the high spots.

Some artists feel that if a palette knife is used at all, the whole picture should be done with a knife, for the sake of consistency in the treatment, and, equally, that if a brush is used the painting should be all with a brush. The idea is reasonable, but again it seems to me that it places unnecessary limitations on individual creativeness. There are certainly great contrasts of texture in nature, and I do not see why we may not try to achieve this quality by any means possible.

I have known artists to put sand in the priming medium while repriming old canvases. The object of this was to vary the grain of the canvas, and the beautiful effect in the final work was astonishing.

All sorts of textures may be prepared on the painting surface. They may be built up by patting the underpainting medium onto the canvas with a two- or three-inch housepainter's brush, lifting the brush, and allowing the textures created by the suction of the brush to stay and dry that way. Should texture not be wanted in some areas, the paint can be sanded down or scraped away with a sharp knife. Modern artists often paint several layers of color on the canvas ground, allowing each layer to dry before applying the next, and then they scrape or sand the surface so that many subtle colors show through. Frequently the resulting effect suggests an abstract composition that can be developed into an interesting design.

121

Paysage du Midi by **André Derain**, BIGNOU GALLERY, NEW YORK CITY.   Some of the most interesting textures in painting can be achieved **by** using a palette knife, dragging the knife over the surface and letting the paint cling to the high spots

Les Mouettes by Henri Matisse, LEWISOHN COLLECTION

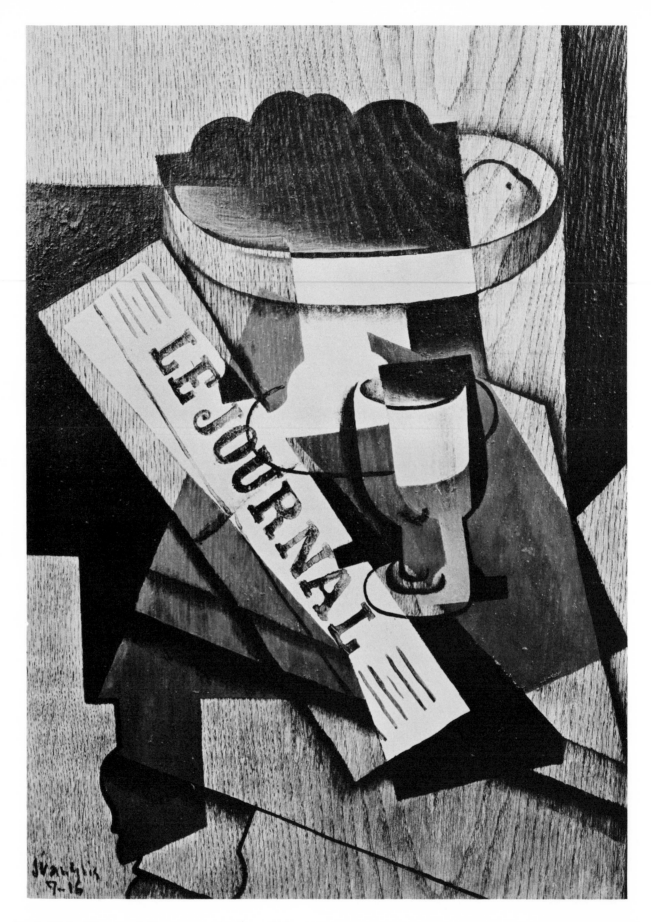

Fruit Dish, Glass and Newspaper by Juan Gris, THE MUSEUM OF MODERN ART, NEW YORK CITY
Texture in painting does not necessarily mean that the surface has to be built up with layers of paint
. . . so the ground cannot show through

TEXTURE

Texture in painting is very much a matter of personal taste. In this, as in every other aspect, the individual artist must be prepared to experiment. Since each applies paint in his own particular way, so will his method of building up texture vary.

Besides underpainting, the use of different types of brushes plays an important part in reproducing the smooth and rough textures found in nature. The over-all effect produced by sable brushes is quite different from that of bristle brushes, and that of round brushes from that of flat or square ones. Some artists paint with the flat of the brush, often brushing sideways rather than off the tip to increase the area covered at one time. Others retain the blocky squareness left by the square brush stroke. Experiments with many textures of paint and with all types of brushes held at all possible angles and with different manipulation of wrist and arm reveal the almost limitless textural effects that can be achieved with paint or canvas.

When you find yourself, your technical approach becomes more or less a habit. This can be good, and it also can be bad. It is good in that it helps to identify your work as you become known. It is definitely bad in that painting habits too deeply ingrained can become monotonous and be difficult to change when a fresh approach is needed. One remedy lies in constant experiment and another in frequent if only temporary changes of locale, where new places and people and collections of art can provide new inspiration and a fresh point of view. This in turn may give birth to interesting new techniques and uses of color.

XI. VALUES OF LIGHT

The intrinsic quality of a painting, taking everything into account, is chiefly determined by the quality of the light. This quality, of course, is the result of a combination of factors in the whole execution of the subject, but its importance lies in the fact that it gives existence to the picture in relation to life itself. When the light is right we never question a painting's reason for being.

In order to achieve such quality we must focus our attention on light itself. This means that we will not be painting the objects before us so much as we will be painting light and the way it falls on these objects or brings them into our vision.

A fine painter once said, "A head is something you choose for the light to fall upon." He meant that a portrait is not a portrait until it exists in light. The life-giving effects of light are far more important than wrinkles in flesh. How few portraits really exist as people, rather than as paintings? How few paintings of any kind exist as anything but paintings?

Vermeer must be credited with being one of the first real painters of light. Though his work seems full of detail and precision, close study reveals that all detail has been subordinated to his one great aim, the interpretation of light. No detail exists where its value might encroach upon the feeling of light on the surface. Although color exists mostly in the light, it must never be allowed to reduce the value of the light. Every lighted area in a picture bears a scaled relationship of both value and color from the lightest area to the darkest area appearing within the light. All else

is shadow, and all the shadows bear a sequence relationship to the lighted areas. When an area in the light is lowered in value, the shadow must be lowered correspondingly. Thus both the light areas and the shadow areas are painted in sequence from lightest to darkest. These two sequences are separated by a degree of contrast determined by the brilliancy of the light itself. Thus contrast makes evident the separation of the whole set of lights from the whole set of shadows. In a dim light this separation may be only one or two tones. In a strong light the lights may be separated from the shadows by three or four tones.

So we must analyze our subject in order to determine the over-all or general relationship of light to shadow. How much darker is the shadow area on that object than the light area? If we decide it is two, three, or even four values darker we accept this as our light-to-shadow scale throughout the picture. Thus all shadows will be the same number of values darker than the value in the light. Since we are limited to eight or at most ten values in our pigment, we may find that some shadows reach the bottom of the scale before we have reached the full scale of values in the lighted areas; that is, we may have a value in the light so low in tone that we cannot produce a value three or four tones lower. This is what is meant by "sacrificing at the low end of the scale." It really does not matter, since we cannot see below black.

Once the over-all relationship is established,

The Pearl Necklace by Jan Vermeer, NATIONAL GALLERY OF ART, WASHINGTON, D. C.   Vermeer must be credited
with being one of the first real painters of light. Though his work seems full of detail and precision, close study
reveals that all detail has been subordinated to his one great aim, the interpretation of light

THE BASIC VALUES OF THE LANDSCAPE

1. When you are looking into the light, the sky is painted as light as possible. All other values are painted a tone or two lower than you see them.

2. Sidelight: sky is the lightest, the ground next, uprights next. Paint lighted areas somewhat lighter and shadows just a bit darker than seen.

3. Looking with the light: sky lowered for brightness of clouds. Ground is slightly lower in tone than sky. The values are closer, softer.

We must remember that our pigment range of light to dark is very much less than the range we see in life. Our only chance to retain the brilliancy and contrast of the lights to the darks is to drop the middle tones and darks in value. In Number 1 the ground plane lightens as it recedes. In Number 2 it lightens from right to left. In 3 the ground lightens as it comes forward. This is important in landscape.

Working against the light produces strong contrast. Working with the light produces close values within the patterns. However, the patterns may contrast.

1. When white areas such as buildings, roads, rocks, sand, or clouds exist in your subject, all other values will usually have to be lowered in order to provide enough contrast.

2. In a side lighting the sky is lighter than when the source is behind you. The shadows are darker than the sky or ground. The values are painted about as you see them.

3. Against the light the white drops below the sky in tone. Study carefully to establish the whole relationship of the sky to the rest of your subject. "Skies make the picture."

Acquainting oneself with the changes of value that come to the same material on different days, or even within the same day, becomes a fascinating study. When we manipulate values, we are seeking the larger truths within our pigmentary limitations, just as we stop down a camera lens for values.

Portrait of an Old Man by Andrew Loomis

The Cove by Andrew Loomis

you will begin to see your painting take on light.

I should perhaps qualify my statement that the degree of difference between light and shadow will be the same for all shadows, for there is an exception in the case of reflected light thrown back into the shadow. The original separation would be correct if we were to take away the source of the reflected light. But the value of a shadow on which light is reflected is of course higher than that of the other shadows. It is very important to study how much the value has been raised. Also, has the whole value of the whole shadow been raised? Most often traces of the original value are left at the edges, between the lighted area and the shadow. This is what artists call the "hump" (the turning point of the form), which the reflected light may not be able to reach. To most artists, reflected light on shadow is a delight to paint, for it gives great luminosity to the shadow. If we paint reflected light too light, it cuts down the brilliance of the neighboring area of light. Sometimes reflected light in a warm light is even warmer in the shadow than it is in the light, for it is color reflected back upon itself. This is what makes the shadows in a flower so brilliant. The pink of a rose seems more brilliant in the shadows between the petals than it does in the light on the petals. This is a perfect example of color radiances, and we should strive to include a similar effect around the lighted areas of our paintings.

Values can be analyzed by comparison. Look for the lightest area in the light, then for the next lower value, and on down the scale. Then look for the degree of contrast between the lightest area and its shadow. Set the value of this shadow down beside the lightest area. It is at the top of the value scale for the shadows, and all other shadows are lowered in the same ratio with the scale of values in the light, keeping the same degree of contrast.

If this is not clear, some comparisons may help. On the piano the relationship of E to G is the same as that of D to F; both are two notes apart, but the latter is lower in scale. The number 3 has the same relationship to 5 as 2 has to 4; they are both two units apart, but the latter are less in amount.

If you number the areas in your drawing, making the lightest 1, and the next 2, the scale would run like this:

Light	Shadow (two tones darker than the light)
1. Highest value	3. Lightest value
2. Next	4. Next
3. Next	5. Next
4. Next	6. Next
5. Next	7. Next
6. Next	8. Next

It is a good idea to mix a black-and-white scale along a flat stick and use this alongside your color palette to determine what the values of the various colors are in terms of black-and-white. In this manner you build the value scales in your picture according to the black-and-white scale, or as they would appear in a black-and-white photograph, and then transpose the correct value to color by means of your value stick. Color can be very deceptive as to value. Because it is vivid, we are inclined to think it lighter than it really is. That is why the black-and-white value scale is so helpful.

If you compare your value scale to nature you will no doubt find that the whole range of the scale is lower than the colors appear in actual light. That is what is meant by the limitation of pigment values. Our white is not as bright as sunlight. All we can do is to try to find the relationships from lightest to darkest and paint them in that order, even if a value has to be painted lower than we see it to keep it in scale.

Much painting lacks quality because the artist does not fully understand the value limitations of his pigments. Instead of arranging his values in proper sequence, he gets some lighter than nature, some like nature, some darker than nature, and so produces incorrect degrees of contrast in his work. His picture appears dull, and he does not

THREE TONES ON WHITE

THREE TONES ON LIGHT GRAY

THREE TONES ON DARK GRAY

THREE TONES ON BLACK

THE FOUR BASIC TONAL ARRANGEMENTS

Consider your subject as made up of four basic patterns of light, light gray, dark gray, and dark. One of these values should dominate the rest. In the simple diagrams above, four values in combination with four different backgrounds are shown, in each case with a different value predominating. The four arrangements can be varied infinitely according to subject, area, and distribution of pattern and pattern shapes. The extreme lights and darks may be reserved for highlights and dark accents. You can experiment with toned papers, chalk, and charcoal, to develop your sense of values and pattern arrangement.

quite know why or what to do about it. Quality must come from relationships which in turn express the true feeling of light.

It is evident from this that a fine painting may not always have true values, since we cannot reach them, but does have true relationships and sequences of values. It took me a long time to find this out, for how could we paint true values when we cannot reach them in pigment? This is what some of the impressionists went after, on the theory that scintillating color applied thickly would reach out into the light and so raise its value, as it unquestionably does. Therefore their pictures contained a new brilliance, which made the thinly painted, smooth pictures of their contemporaries look dull and dark by comparison. Strangely enough, the technique of using paint so it catches more light, and therefore increasing the value range of the pigment, was considered a trick when it was first tried.

Relating the sequences of values according to the way the eye would see them often adds a feeling of elegance that can be achieved in no other way. I feel that much of the elegance in Sargent's portraits can be attributed to this, apart from his models and materials. Let us say that he painted elegantly the elegance of his time.

But we can, through color and values, attach elegance to the commonplace. Part of the revolt of modern art is against the wrong sort of elegance. There is a difference between true elegance and insipid formality. We certainly cannot supplant elegance with either mediocrity or the grotesque. We cannot ignore craftsmanship in art and relegate it to the past.

There are various qualities of light itself that must be considered. Let us understand how light truly operates. When there is strong light from a concentrated or condensed source, then light casts shadows. The more condensed the source, the sharper the shadow; also, the closer to the source the sharper the shadow. The more brilliant the light, the darker the shadow by contrast. This is our means of obtaining brilliance, the contrast of light and shadow. But we can work only one way, which is downward from white. So to paint bright light we must use more tonal difference between light and shadow, because the darker the shadow the brighter our top values in the light appear by sheer contrast.

When the light source is not condensed but is spread over a large area—like the sky, or the north light in a window—there is diffused shadow. Shadow in diffused light does exist, but only a sharp turn in the plane can give this type of shadow a sharp edge. On a flat surface the shadow simply diffuses into the light. When we throw light on the ceiling, the ceiling then becomes the light source of the room, and the effect is diffused light, similar to that from a cloudy sky. The rays are not condensed or concentrated as they are from the sun, from a searchlight, or even from an electric bulb, so the whole lighting becomes soft. Surface texture becomes less evident. Soft light is flattering to the face, because in it the face shows as tone rather than as plane, texture, and detail. But diffused light does the same thing to all form. Things are seen in mass and simple tone. Consistency of all the forms affected by such diffusion of light and shadow, with the proper sequence of value and color, lends elegance to the picture. Such a picture will harmonize with any interior where diffused light is used, whether it is a gallery or a home.

Diffusion also results from the use of a great many lights which intermingle their rays. This accounts for the softness of many photographic portraits. Here the photographer keeps filling in lights until cast shadows apparently disappear. The single source of light, by contrast, produces more solidity of form, since the form becomes evident through the planes of light, halftone, and shadow.

Rembrandt and other Dutch painters purposely cut their light down to a small opening in order to concentrate light where they wanted it. This was how Rembrandt caused his figures to loom mysteriously out of darkness, but such

Man with a Magnifying Glass by Rembrandt, METROPOLITAN MUSEUM
OF ART, NEW YORK CITY

The Twelfth Night Feast by Jan Steen, THE CLEVELAND MUSEUM OF
ART, CLEVELAND

Rembrandt and other Dutch painters purposely cut their light down
to a small opening in order to concentrate light where they wanted it.
This was how Rembrandt caused his figures to loom mysteriously out
of darkness, but such concentration also resulted in more solid form

concentration also resulted in more solid form.

In photography we get a sharper picture when we cut down the aperture in a camera and increase the exposure time. When we want softness, we open the aperture wide and shorten the exposure. This lesson in the way light operates can be used to advantage in painting—for a soft picture, a wide source of light; for a sharp and brilliant picture, a concentrated source. In many subjects the right choice of lighting can make an immense difference in the quality.

There are considerations in lighting besides sharpness or diffusion: for instance, the color of the light itself, and, with brilliant concentrated light, the direction from which light comes. If we paint light correctly, the form will take care of itself. We simply state the lights, halftones, and shadows as they occur and where they occur. We have to worry only about correct sequences of value relationships and about getting the color safely within these values.

The reverse is also true: if we paint the form correctly in value and color, and on the proper planes, the brilliancy and beauty of the light will take care of itself.

Light and its effects provide the best means of bringing unity and consistency to a subject. Since the same light falls on everything in the subject, from the same direction, everything takes its relative place in the whole scheme, and all colors and values are brought together into a single effect. This unity is the first essential of true beauty.

XII. BEAUTY OF SUBJECT

In painting for beauty we have two courses open to us. One is to give a beautiful interpretation and rendering of a subject, regardless of the material, and the other is to seek material which we consider beautiful in itself. The latter seems the more obvious choice. But what counts in the end is the amount of beauty the artist can see and interpret.

Among the work of the great masters we find the extremes. Rubens sought beauty on a grandiose scale while Chardin, for instance, with his still lifes, sought beauty in a simple loaf of bread. We visualize Rubens in a huge studio, filled with gorgeous accessories and enormous canvases, with a bevy of helpers grinding his paints, building scaffolds, and possibly even laying in the groundwork of his paintings. We think of Chardin as sitting by the window of his bedroom, a few objects set on a table before him. But both of these men created immortal works.

In the choice of subjects, a time may come when the artist begins to be governed by his technical skill. There are certain things he likes to paint, not so much for themselves as because they are suited to his technique. There are certain types of lighting that he has mastered. And he may simply have learned to find material that adapts itself to his way of painting. This probably comes largely as the result of experiment, through which he has found out also what kind of subjects give him most trouble. Though it is advisable to continue to experiment and seek to analyze new problems, when a man is painting for his own

satisfaction he is entitled to choose subjects that give him the greatest joy to interpret. However the danger that lies in continually choosing the same kind of subject is that the artist may narrow his approach and fail to grow in stature. Or he may merely grow stale.

Since we paint light and form in the same way, it should not make too much difference what the form is, or what material it is composed of. A man can find as much pleasure in painting the planes, values, and colors of a rock as he can in painting flesh. I have heard instructors advise their students to look at all material with a cold, dispassionate eye, on the theory that if we get the form and color we get all there is to paint. This seems a little too methodical to me. It puts too much stress on craftsmanship and not enough on emotion. It might work if all we intend to do is copy what we see, but to me a painting becomes art only when we recognize and stress the qualities that move us and stir our enthusiasm. A personal response is needed to create an individual expression.

Everyone must choose subjects that excite him and immediately make him want to paint them. He can only do that by getting out of the studio, seeing more, taking trips, doing things that might turn up material. Edward Hopper travels widely in search of subjects that interest him—an old gingerbread house, a bit of landscape. And so do most other artists.

No vacation should be embarked upon without a sketch pad and a color camera. There are al-

Rubens sought beauty on a grandiose scale

Venus and Adonis by Peter Paul Rubens, METROPOLITAN MUSEUM OF ART, NEW YORK CITY.

ways worth-while subjects to paint and sometimes we are lucky enough to be at hand when a spectacular effect or event occurs. We used to be told to avoid the spectacular, such as blazing sunset effects, waterfalls, storms, or the brilliance of the sun against the dark clouds as a storm retreats. But perhaps the time has come for the painter of realism to be a little more spectacular. Why not paint the unusual if it strikes you as beautiful? Perhaps a shaft of brilliant sunlight makes a daring and striking composition, something arresting that you have never seen painted before. Have the courage to try it. When we look at the daring of the modernists, anything the realistic painter might do must seem much tamer by comparison than it would have done in the past. Good taste can have force and vitality. It need not always be sedate and clothed in dignity. If a bullfight or the prize ring appeals to an artist, why should he not transfer some of the attendant excitement to his canvas?

While it is true that something peaceful and pleasant might be easier to live with, the tempo of life today is not the peaceful seclusion of the life of yesterday. We need not resort to shock tactics, but some of the excitement of modern life should be introduced into our work.

Beauty of subject is not limited to realism, modernism, or any other school. If you can produce beauty by pouring paint on the canvas, I say do it. But make beauty as *you* see it your goal. There is as much inward joy in creating beauty as in finding it.

Sooner or later every artist has to find an au-dience for his paintings. Otherwise he continues to work in a sort of vacuum. While at first he can paint for himself, the time comes when he must feel his work is appreciated, if not by the many, then at least by the few. If we can find out what people love, and interpret these things pictorially, we have made a long step toward having our work accepted. Some of these things are material, some are more or less intangible and abstract, and some are purely spiritual.

Man is motivated to a large extent by experience and memory. He is more inclined to remember happy experiences than unhappy ones. The latter he prefers to forget. A man who has happy memories of open country in his boyhood will probably like paintings of landscape. The boy who grew up on a farm will no doubt react to farm scenes, cattle, horses, and other animals. The boy who went sailing grows into a man who loves marines and sailboats. The small-town boy probably likes "homey" subjects, the corner drugstore, the circus, the town hall, the village nestled in the hills. A man will like pictures that are related to his hopes, his ambitions, his life, and his loves. The appeal of portraits is perhaps the most self-evident.

People are not likely to change greatly in their basic habitual likes and dislikes, no matter what kind of art is served to them. They will always be motivated by basic emotions, memories, and associations of personal experiences. When we can add technical beauty to something which is already appealing in its nature, we double the response of the viewer.

XIII. TECHNIQUE

Technique contributes much to the inherent beauty of a painting. But it is a result rather than a conscious procedure. Unless an artist understands tone, color, and form, technique can do little for him. But a rich technique which incorporates those qualities can call attention to an artist's individuality and make his work recognizable.

Imitation does not pay, no matter what the temptation. We all tend to like another man's work better than our own. What we do not know is that he may struggle just as much with his work as we do with ours. After our own struggles, our work may look worse to us than it does to others. We remember all the frustrations we have had in producing it. The artist himself is usually the last man capable of fair criticism of his own work.

Technique, then, provides the main opportunity for individuality. But the technique must be in the whole approach rather than a matter of tricks. Tricks can be copied, but never a whole approach, for the imitator has not the same knowledge, the same preferences, the same sense of design and color, or the same responses.

There are many effects of technique which the artist may use when they actually contribute to a whole effect. There is no real need of limiting oneself to a single technique. Do not say, "This is it, I will do it this way forever." That leaves no room for further discovery.

There are a few methods of putting on paint which may open new doors later when you are looking for a fresh approach.

There are two ways to go around a form, laterally or crosswise, and vertically or up and down. The first seems to be best done with small strokes, the latter with wider, simpler strokes. Zuloaga and Tito, Benson and Tarbell are good examples of the lateral method, and Sargent of the vertical. In both cases the strokes are left in evidence. Van Gogh employed small strokes in all directions. These approaches result in very different technical character in paintings. You can go across the edge to produce softness and along the edge to produce sharpness and precision. Some painters apply both techniques, and the combination can be very pleasing.

The small stroke used laterally permits much more use of color, especially broken color. The up-and-down permits less color but much more decided stressing of form.

There is another approach in which the whole plane of the form is brushed in, usually with the side of the brush, and the value and color is quite flat until it meets the next plane. This approach was used very beautifully by Charles Hawthorne.

Then there is the approach which leaves little or no evidence of the brush stroke, except in accents and highlights, the rest being kept quite smooth and flat with considerable merging of tone and plane. This amounts to a very soft underpainting with all the crispness in the accents. The edges are quite sharp where there is contrast of tone and very soft where the values are close.

Since technique is so much a matter of individual approach, some artists go so far as to say

138

that technique should never be taught, that the student should be free to develop his own from the start. This might work with students who were well grounded in the other fundamentals of drawing—design and values. There is hardly a chance of developing well-founded and good technique until these fundamentals are fairly well mastered. Only then will the need for an individual technical approach begin to show. Normally the difficulties caused by insufficient knowledge of the fundamentals lead to so much going over and repainting that any technical unity becomes lost. Paint begins to get tacky; values become muddy because dark undertones come up through the lighter tones; and lack of experience in handling the medium plays havoc with the subject so far as any clean color and directness is concerned. The artist has to learn gradually to work in steps, having the final effects in mind as he lays in the first color. These difficulties in connection with the medium of oil send many a student to water color, either transparent or opaque, which has the property of drying faster and is more manageable by the inexperienced.

There are several easier mediums for the beginner than oil paint. They can be classified as wet and dry. Dry mediums, so called since they are the most part worked over a dry surface, include pastels, colored pencil, oil chalks, and at times tempera and watercolor. Even though a watercolor is wet at the time of application, much of the painting is done with wet tones over dry tones. With oil, however, most of the painting is wet paint painted into wet, except when a subject has been deliberately set aside to allow the paint to dry and wet paint is later dragged over the dry surface. The watercolorist can also get many of his best effects by painting wet color into wet or dampened surfaces. Some even keep a wet blotter under the watercolor paper to hold the dampness and allow painting of wet into wet over a longer period. The finishing is then done over a dry surface.

Oil paint, by and large, seems to be the most profound of mediums in the hands of the experienced, since it is the most flexible in regard to manipulation and change and at the same time the most durable and unfading. Perhaps because of its association with fine art through all the different periods of art, oil color seems to bring the highest prices of all mediums.

There are those who prefer to start their subjects in tempera and finish up with oil paint. This can give a great richness of effect. Some artists even start their canvases in a monotone of warm black to establish the patterns and values, and then match these values in color over the black-and-white underpainting. This is an excellent way of getting good values. However, unless the underpainting has had time to dry thoroughly, the black can easily work up through the color and muddy it. Such paintings also have a tendency to darken with time, unless the overpainting is thick enough to prevent any transparency from developing later on. This is much like matching values with color over a photograph, but that should be done only for practice and matching values.

Here again I might mention the practice of applying an undertone of gray or of a color to the white canvas, in order to determine the values more easily.

Another practice worth experimentation is drawing in the subject with thin washes of blue and then filling in the dark areas with strong blue before overpainting in a warmer color. Warm dark color painted over cool colors gives a desirable vibration to areas which are to be kept dark in the painting. Conversely, in areas that are to be kept light, cool color painted over warm seems richer than warm colors over cool. Often a blue sky can be painted over a warm undertone, with much more vitality than just the blue paint on white canvas gives.

No one can tell the student what kind of technique he should eventually develop, but it is helpful to suggest experiments from which he can choose his own course. Too many instructors teach their own style of approach instead of allowing experimentation. This may serve a purpose in developing at least one approach by which the work can be carried through to a good finish. But it is questionable whether most students will thereafter experiment themselves. They are more likely to think they have learned to paint and have acquired all the technical know-how they need.

There is a theory that if the student pays no attention whatever to technique, he will probably develop his own style. There is much truth in this, but it implies a great deal of native ability and imagination. I do not know any artist who, in his student days and even during his professional output, has not been influenced many times over by the work of others. The very basis on which an artist works is doing what he likes most. If he likes another man's work it helps him to shape his own opinions. This inevitably and sometimes unconsciously leads to the temptation to imitate. If he realizes it, he can set a limit for himself and make sure that he goes to the source before he gets too deep in imitation. If the man he admires could make something individual, he can also. A particular technique rightfully belongs only to the man who invents it, except when enough individual variation can evolve a different technique from it. Short strokes and long strokes, as well as edges and accents, are any artist's property. But copying a man's mannerisms and individual style is like lifting his wallet from his pocket.

The preparation of painting surfaces, previously mentioned, has much to do with technical effect. There are so many possibilities here that no one needs to imitate.

A fast-drying white will give a very different effect in the application of paint than a slow-drying one. The same is true of a thick, heavy white as contrasted to a softer, more buttery one. Both kinds of white may be used in the same subject, so long as the whites are the same chemically. A fast-drying white may be mixed with a slow-drying white of the same chemical compound, to hasten the slow one or to slow down the fast one. The slowing process is very welcome at times, since underpainting may set and get tacky before one has a chance to get it all down.

Brushes make a considerable difference in technical effect. Where flatness or smoothness is desired, the sable brush does a better job than the bristle. Where paint texture is desired, bristle brushes are best. Square brushes produce a very different technique from that produced by round or long bristles. Different types of brushes may be used in the same subject for different effects.

The artists' supply houses provide a great variety of materials with which to experiment. As a painting surface, for example, Masonite is much cheaper than canvas, and can be sized with any kind of surface you like. To those who do not mind having no "give" to the painting surface, Masonite makes a durable and long-lasting base for a painting. Some painters, however, prefer the resiliency of canvas.

There is a technical effect wherein the canvas is not solidly covered and bits of the bare canvas are allowed to show through. This is especially effective in high-keyed pictures. It keeps the subject sketchy and loose, as in the first lay-in of a painting. But it should be fairly consistent throughout the subject, or one area may appear spotty while another is painted in solidly, and the picture appears to be unfinished. This type of approach has been used effectively by Augustus John, among others.

In another approach, the paint is laid on very thickly, almost as if the tube itself had been pressed against the canvas, or the brush loaded, and the paint left untouched as it falls on the canvas. Examples of this approach are the work of John Costigan, William Redfield, and the paintings of the New England school. It is really derived from the French impressionists.

The "square-brush" approach is a very virile and effective one. Examples may be found in the work of Abbot Thayer, Robert Henri, Frank Duveneck, and others.

Portrait of Madame Monet and Bazille by Claude Monet, NATIONAL GALLERY OF ART, WASHINGTON, D. C. In another approach, the paint is laid on very thickly, almost as if the tube itself had been pressed against the canvas, or the brush loaded, and the paint left untouched as it falls on the canvas. . . . It is really derived from the French impressionists

141

THE EYE OF THE PAINTER

There is a very wonderful approach which is found at its best in the work of Toulouse-Lautrec. The canvas has a feeling of a color drawing on a tone but vibrates with color. Most of Toulouse-Lautrec's work was done in pastel, but the approach has also been used with tempera and oil.

Experiment with all these approaches will help the student find himself. I believe every artist must go through a period of "feeling out" his talent and ability to find their best expression. Each must keep his own eyes and ears open for any means to give his work greater beauty. Let him learn as much about art generally as he can absorb, and his later work will take care of itself.

Nothing is quite so fascinating as to get off on a new track, to try a new kind of approach. It is not enough to choose a variety of subjects, if you treat them all in the same way. Experimenting keeps your work young and your enthusiasm working as nothing else can.

All creative endeavor has its technique. In the broad sense technique covers method and application of knowledge as well as dexterity in the handling of material. I have placed technique last in the list of the elements of beauty because I think of it as a summing up and a combination of all the other elements. From this standpoint no two works of art can ever have exactly the same technical approach.

When you are not quite sure what you want to do with a subject, small preliminary studies or sketches will help you decide and so add directness in the final work. It is strange how much direction of execution can contribute to any effort. In business it may make the difference which causes one man to be promoted instead of another. The faltering individual may actually know more, but the job usually goes to the man who is decisive. We sense faltering in a work of art as quickly as in any other expression. In painting, much uncertainty may be avoided by knowing and planning your subject thoroughly. Do not start your subject until you have gathered together all the necessary working material. Know your forms from having drawn them carefully beforehand. Be decided about your patterns and composition from having tried them out in sketch form. Be sure you are lighting your material consistently throughout. Try out your color separately first so that it goes down freshly and directly.

In this way, you leave the smallest possible margin for error. When art fails, nine times out of ten it fails for lack of preparation, just as anything else does. The good speaker is usually the one who has prepared his talk, or at least knows thoroughly what he is talking about. Impromptu art seldom clicks any better than an impromptu speech does.

We hear much from the layman about painters with "natural-born" ability. On investigation they usually prove rather to be self-taught, to have expended much effort on their own in acquiring what they know. Real skill rarely comes without effort, though it may often appear to do so.

In the end every artist must teach himself most of what he knows, whether he has instructors or learns from books or observation. However he gains his information, he constantly applies and experiments with it.

George Bridgman, who taught not only drawing but anatomy, once said to me: "Son, if you are having trouble drawing hands, you have the best instructor with you at all times, your own hands!" Of course this is true, for you can measure the comparative proportions of the fingers to the palm, the shape and paddings of the palm, and the placement of bones and knuckles in relation to one another.

This thought can be extended much further. The facts that we need to solve any problem are right before us and have been all the time. It simply doesn't occur to us that knowledge is simply a matter of getting acquainted with them. Only our own eyes and brains can actually teach us anything. At best instructors can only show us how to see for ourselves and so start us on our own search for truth.

Talent is really a capacity for a certain type

There is a very wonderful approach which is found at its best in the work of Toulouse-Lautrec. The canvas has a feeling of a color drawing on a tone but vibrates with color

At the Moulin Rouge by Henri Toulouse-Lautrec, THE ART INSTITUTE OF CHICAGO, CHICAGO.

143

of knowledge and a consuming interest in the facts that contribute to that knowledge. It is significant that those who acquire knowledge easily seldom make as good use of it later on as those who had to work hard to acquire it. I think the reason may be that the former do not attach as much importance to the knowledge. I remember "stars" in my classes who were never heard from later. But the strugglers and hard workers all seemed to come through.

There is such a great difference between theory and practice. We must have theory, but it is worth little until we have proved the theory to ourselves by actual practice. But constant practice also means little unless you keep adding to your working knowledge. Doing the same thing over and over without acquiring new facts between efforts also accomplishes very little. Unfortunately this happens all the time, and nothing is so discouraging. We must spend as much time seeking the "whys" as in doing the job. There is always a source if we have the patience to seek it out. We cannot just hope for miracles, we must somehow make them.